Measured Expectations

The Challenges of Today's Freemasonry

A Cornerstone Book

Measured Expectations
The Challenges of Today's Freemasonry
by Michael R. Poll

A Cornerstone Book
Published by Cornerstone Book Publishers

Back Cover Portrait by Travis Simpkins
http://www.artcrimeillustrated.com

Views expressed in this publication are those of Michael R. Poll and not necessarily those of any Masonic Body. Comments on Masonic procedure are given from the perspective of the Grand Lodge of Louisiana and may, or may not, reflect those of other jurisdictions.

Cornerstone Book Publishers
New Orleans, LA

First Cornerstone Edition - 2017

www.cornerstonepublishers.com

ISBN:1613422946
ISBN-13:978-1-61342-294-6

MADE IN THE USA

Table of Contents

Introduction

A few years ago I was enjoying a nice meal at a Lodge just prior to their meeting. It was the Lodge's celebration of their 25 and 50 year Masons. I was sitting at a table with one of Brothers who was to receive his 25 Year Certificate. He was a Past Master of the Lodge. He was telling me that I should not expect much in the way of any sort of presentation as the Lodge always did a horrible job with such events. In an off-hand manner, I mentioned that this is something that the Lodge should practice. He said that in order to practice, someone would have to know what to do so that he can show the others. He said that as long as he has been a member, no one teaches anything in the Lodge because no one knows anything. He said that the Masonic books that he has read all seem to assume that everyone knows the basics of Lodge operation. He said that either the books assume too much or are written in such a "high brow" manner that no one can understand them. That conversation gave me cause to do a considerable bit of thinking. The result is this offering of mine.

This book is designed to be something of a beginners guide to "doing things" in Masonry as well as a bit of plain talk regarding some of our teachings. I've tried to include thoughts that touch on the basics of Lodge operation, laws, practices, and a bit of the nature of Freemasonry. These are aspects that I believe should be known by Masons no matter if they are new or if they have been around for a while.

I truly believe that if we keep reaching up to the Light, we can achieve far more than we might realize.

Lux E Tenebris.

Michael R. Poll

June, 2017

Measured Expectations
The Challenges of Today's Freemasonry

A Young Man Joins a Masonic Lodge

Not long ago, a young man turned in his petition to a Masonic Lodge. Maybe a relative of his was a Mason, or maybe he learned of Freemasonry from a popular book or movie. Regardless, he expressed his desire to join.

A few weeks after turning in his petition, he received a phone call from a man who told him that he was a member of an investigation committee working on the petition. He asked the young man if he and two other Lodge members could come to his house to meet with him. They met at the appointed time. It was a good meeting. Questions were asked, and everyone learned a bit more of each other.

The committee told the young man that Freemasonry is not an insurance agency. Masonry does not extend health benefits nor give promises of financial assistance. While Lodges and individual Freemasons have a long and honorable history of assisting those in need, Freemasonry is not designed to be a charitable organization, such as the Red Cross.

Freemasonry is also not a civic association such as the Jaycees or Lions Club. The primary goal of Freemasonry is to take good men and, through moral instruction, give them the keys by which they can, hopefully, make themselves better and happier in their lives.

The young man took in all that he was told. He then asked about the history of Freemasonry. He was told that we don't have a complete or clear understanding of all aspects of our beginnings. We know that we are old. As an organization, we go back to around 1717 with the reported creation of the Grand Lodge of England. But many claim that we can trace ourselves to much earlier times – to the days of the old Operative Freemasons. Many also claim that we can trace our philosophy and manner of symbolic education to an even much earlier time. Sadly, we just don't have definitive answers. The young petitioner accepted all that he was told, and the committee left. Both sides were satisfied.

The young man was quietly excited. He knew that what he wanted to join was something very old and very important. He couldn't explain why, but he felt it in his heart. He had done his homework. He had already read the popular books and conducted internet searches of Freemasonry. He knew better than to pay attention to the large amount of flash concerning Freemasonry. He ignored the wild supernatural claims and nonsensical satanic charges. But, he knew that there was something very special about Freemasonry, its manner of instruction by degrees, and the whole Masonic philosophy. He felt very good about joining.

In a few weeks, a letter came in the mail telling him that the Lodge had voted on his petition. The ballot was clear, and the date of the initiation set. But, there were many questions that he had forgotten to ask. One thing that he was unsure about was how he should dress for the initiation. He thought about calling, but then remembered some of the books he owned. In them the Masons all wore business suits and some even wore tuxedoes. The photos were not all that old, so he thought that he should try to match their dress. He knew that this was something special, but assumed that if they wanted him to wear a tux, they would have told him. So, he decided to wear his suit.

When he showed up at the lodge, a number of the members were wearing old blue jeans and equally faded and worn polo shirts — some t-shirts. Others looked like they were wearing soiled work clothes and had come directly to lodge from work. He felt a bit out of place in such a casual atmosphere. One of the men laughed when he saw him and asked if he was going to church or a wedding.

The young man waited downstairs and was finally called up for the initiation. He felt slightly uncomfortable as the man who came down for him was laughing and told him, "Now you are in for it!" In for what? What did he mean by that?

He was placed in a little room by a kindly, elderly man who seemed sincerely interested in his well-being. This made him feel better. The degree began.

After the degree ended, the young man had mixed emotions. He knew that what he had experienced was something very important, but why was there so much laughter and talking going on? Why did he hear a considerable amount of yelling out instructions? It was clear that some who spoke did not, at all, know their lines (they were stumbling and fumbling over every few words) and others, from everywhere, were telling the officers what to say (and, loudly).

As he was walking around, he also heard about someone's wife being sick and another's cousin who is building a new garage. What did all that have to do with his degree? But afterwards, everyone was so friendly. Maybe he expected too much. Maybe Freemasonry really is just a group of men who meet to enjoy themselves and try to do antiquated and meaningless ritual every now and then.

In time, the young man's feelings about Masonry changed from those prior to his joining. These were all nice guys. Every time he went to a meeting, he was greeted with smiles, friendly handshakes, and inquiries of his health and well-being.

There was a mixture of blue collar workers and professional men. All seemed truly interested in the lodge, but most could not really answer even the most basic questions concerning Freemasonry. It was almost as if Freemasonry and the lodge were two completely different things.

Questions on the ritual or history were always passed to one brother who they said was the "answer man." They were a nice group of men – friends – but there was nothing *special* in the lodge; special in the way he viewed Masonry before he joined. This was a club made up of good guys who would meet a couple of times a month to enjoy themselves. They would visit and share a few laughs during a friendly evening. That seemed to be all that he could expect from the lodge experience. The books clearly were speaking of something else. But what? Who were the Freemasons that he had read about? Did they ever exist? Was it all made up to sell books?

After a few months, the young man found that a TV show was scheduled at the same time as his lodge meeting. It was a show that he had wanted to watch for some time. He chose the show over the lodge. Over the next few months and years, it became easier and easier to choose many events over the lodge meetings.

Eventually, the young man attended lodge, maybe, once or twice a year. He made an effort to try to attend some of the important meetings. He did so out of a feeling of obligation, not really enjoyment. He did see some who truly seemed to enjoy each and every meeting. These were the men who kept the lodge alive.

At a few meetings, some of the ones who were always there gently scolded him for not attending more of the lodge functions. "You know, the lodge depends on its members and if you don't support the lodge, it will fail." But, what was he to do? Was he really obligated to continually go to a place that provided him with no benefit at all other than a few laughs and a meal? He had tried, but after many months of only hearing a reading of the last meeting, bills that needed to be paid, who was sick, and discussion of the next planned social event, he grew disinterested. He knew that he could spend his time in more productive ways.

So, was he to be blamed as it was suggested? He even read such things from "ranking" Masons who seemed to put all responsibility for the success or failure of a body on his simply attending, regardless of what was offered. The man at the top was never to blame, and even if he was, nothing was ever done.

There was no accountability for poor leadership. It was always the rank and file members who seemed to be the responsible parties.

The suggestion was that there was some lacking in the young Mason, and he needed to "wake up" then give his total support to whatever was offered.

Was there a lacking in him?

Clearly, Freemasonry either failed this young man in about every way possible or there truly was some lacking in him. Was there a misunderstanding on his part as to the actual nature of Freemasonry? Is Freemasonry only a club made up of good men who try to do charitable work and hold friendly meetings, or is it an organization designed to educate and uplift its members through moral instruction?

In several publications, the young man saw written: "Freemasonry is the world's oldest and largest fraternity. Its history and tradition date to antiquity. Its singular purpose is to make good men better."

Okay, that's clear. But how do we do that?

Since this quote was written in a Masonic education publication, maybe that should give us a clue. We should teach and instruct our candidates. There are countless books and articles written on Masonic education. We learn the importance of education and teaching in our very ritual. But apart from the ritual, do we actually *teach* Freemasonry, or is it only words to be spoken or read and not acted upon?

How many young men are lost to us simply because we fail to do what we say we will do?

William Lowe Bryan (the tenth president of Indiana University) is credited with writing: "Education is one of the few things a person is willing to pay for and not get." I believe this is sometimes very true, and has been for a good number of years, regarding Freemasonry. It seems that the hole that was left when quality education ceased to take place in the lodges may have been replaced with additional fellowship.

That's not a bad thing, but it's not the life blood of Freemasonry. Initiation and making good men "better" is our main reason for existence.

The passing of time is unavoidable. Every year, our lodges hold elections for officers to lead them for the next year. The young men who came into the lodge, but learned very little about Freemasonry, are now in leadership positions. They are the leaders, but truthfully, many are not qualified.

To be fair, it's not really their fault. With the speed many of them go through the chairs, how can they help but be inexperienced? They are where they are because someone tapped them on the shoulder and asked them if they would accept a position. They were just trying to be helpful.

Maybe the lodge felt that it had no one else to ask and had to take whoever it could get. Maybe it was felt that to take anyone, even someone very inexperienced, was better than closing shop.

Where Masonic education once took place, discussions of Lodge picnics or other lodge events are heard at the meetings. The time that was once spent by the Worshipful Master on the planning of the Masonic education of the members is often now spent on trying to learn the very basics of lodge leadership.

Lodge meetings are only as long as felt necessary and then the "enjoyable" time of the lodge takes place — sharing a few laughs with friends. The leaders are expected to keep the members happy, not spend too much money, and get through their year with as little hassle as possible. The "hole" was filled, and we are marking time, just getting through the years.

But marking time and just getting by does not secure the future of Freemasonry. It is not responsible. It is not enough that we *say* that we are "Freemasonry," but act like a club. We must either be what we say, or admit to being something else.

To all the junior officers of Freemasonry, no matter if you are brand new to Freemasonry, or have been a Mason for a number of years and are only now returning to lodge activity; no matter what level of experience and knowledge you have — *stop*. Take a breath. You are not alone. You don't have to have a situation where young men are leaving your lodges because of claims that you are not giving them what they expected. You don't have to worry that you will all of a sudden be in charge and not know what in the world to do or say. You have Brothers who wish to help you.

But just as each of you had to step up and ask to join Freemasonry, you need to step up and make your needs and desires known. And when you are a junior officer is the time when you should do this.

The internet is filled with Masonic education websites, but which are reliable? You may wish to seek out the recognized and respected Masonic education sources. In the U.S., quality Masonic educational/service societies which you can, and should, join such as The Philalethes Society[1]; The Masonic Society[2]; The Masonic Service Association of North America[3] and other worthy state and national organizations are designed to provide quality Masonic educational resources and services.

I believe deeply in the importance of finding balance in everything. Going too far one way or the other never seems to bring about what is truly desired. But what do we do about our present situation? We have already gone too far. Our lodges have taken on more of the appearance of clubs than lodges of moral instruction.

It was not done through maliciousness; it was done out of a desire to help and preserve. It did not happen all at once, but over a period of time. It was done with no ill intentions. We all know that there is a problem in our lodges. We know that they are not the same lodges as before.

We hear the stories of days long gone. Our leaders desire to do good, but some are uncertain as to which path is the best one. None wish for everything to fall apart on their watch. Some may feel that to do nothing is better than to do the wrong thing.

But cancer is never cured by inaction. There is an old Rosicrucian thought that everything felt to be of value must face the test of death. What is truly of value, will come back alive. What is of no value, will fade away.

Is Freemasonry of value?

I do not believe that society (or any group of people) is changed in mass by outside influences. I believe that change always comes through individual change. When we change as individuals, and if others change in a like manner, then society changes. I believe that the very first step we can take is to recognize that we are in trouble and traveling in the wrong direction.

Value is a perception. We place whatever value we choose on something. Value can also change. If you don't treat something as if it is special or valuable, it's not.

Anyone who knows me personally knows that I live in blue jeans. But those who only know me from lodge believe that I live in business suits. Going to lodge is something very special to me. I dress accordingly. If I did not own a suit, I would clean myself and wear the best shirt and slacks I owned.

Try this the next time you visit your lodge: act as if it is a *very* special occasion; as if you are going to a *very* special place to do *very* special things. Do what you would do if you were going to such a special event.

Fix your mind to always treat going to lodge as something *very* important and special. Make that one permanent change in your life. After you have done this, join or take advantage of what is offered in one of the Masonic education services or societies mentioned earlier.

Freemasonry will be what its members make it. The true and sole power within Freemasonry is where it has always been, with its members — with you.

Notes:

1. http://www.freemasonry.org/
2. http://themasonicsociety.com/
3. http://www.msana.com/

Masonic Ritual in the United States

In the United States, there is, for the most part, one accepted craft ritual. It is the ritual, or a version of it, that is worked in the vast majority of the lodges. It is the ritual hammered out by Thomas Smith Webb in the late 1700's. It's known, unofficially, as the "Webb Ritual," the "Preston / Webb Ritual," and even "the American Rite." But in most cases, it is simply known, in the U.S. as "the craft ritual." It is most often called by no name, because a name is not really necessary.

Maybe to better understand the situation, think of a small town where there is only one grocery. The grocery will certainly have a name. It may be named *The Central Grocery*, or *Joe's Grocery*, or whatever name they gave it. But the point is that because there is only one grocery in that town, they can just call it "the grocery." "I'm going to the grocery." Sure, if there were more than one grocery, they would have to identify which grocery, like, "I'm going to *Joe's Grocery*."

This is the same situation that exists in most areas of U.S. Masonry. When we, in the U.S., talk of the craft lodge, we are almost always talking about one ritual and one rite. Further identification is not needed.

Sure, by now, many have heard about those ten Scottish Rite craft lodges under the jurisdiction of the Grand Lodge of Louisiana. But it's a big country, and most everywhere else there is just one ritual.

In his paper, "The Webb Ritual in the United States,"[1] Silas Shepherd tells us of the Masons involved in the development of what would become the ritual used by most all of Masonry in the United States. It is an interesting story and provides details on not only the Webb ritual but the other players and events which had a role in the ritual's development.

It would seem that just following the American War of Independence, Freemasonry in the United States went through something of an identity crisis. The Lodges and provincial Grand Lodges in the new country were cut off from their mother bodies, mostly in the United Kingdom. There was a period of time when it was not certain what would happen with Masonry in the youthful United States of America.

Some felt that maybe there should be one Grand Lodge for the entire country. Suggestions were made that maybe even George Washington should become the first Grand Master. Others felt that if the states were to be truly important pieces in a whole, and that the country was based on the collective authority of the states, then maybe each state should have a sovereign and independent Grand Lodge.

When the debates were over, the new county settled on the concept of one Grand Lodge per state, but they also agreed, in theory, on one ritual per state including the suggestion that they should be one language, which would be English. The idea for Masonry in the United States would seem to be that it was desirous for every state to be independent, but a copy of the other. It would seem that to be like others was good and to be unlike the rest was not good. Over time this concept did create problems.

One problem was that everyone was not alike. Just to give one example, in 1803, the young United States grew in size by almost a third when it obtained from France the massive section of land known as the Louisiana Purchase. At the heart of this purchase was the very important port of New Orleans. But this was a French territory with most of the citizens speaking French and proud to be of French heritage.

Masonry, as best as we can tell, had existed in New Orleans since 1752. Its nature and language matched its members, meaning French. As English speaking, American Masons arrived in the area, they found the Masonry in New Orleans different than that in the rest of the U.S. It became a problem for them and resulted in Masonic conflict for many years to follow. But since we know that more than one Masonic ritual exists in the world, does it help, hurt or not matter at all if we limit our Lodges to only one ritual? In my opinion, and from the standpoint of initiation, it doesn't matter at all. The differences in rituals are all a matter of choice, a matter of preference, or even just what is available in the area. At best, it's all a matter of taste.

The various rituals may have different words, actions, and even different feels to them, but at the heart of them all is the Hiramic Legend. It is that legend and the symbolic teachings woven into it that defines a Masonic initiation from other forms of initiation.

An initiation is not considered valid because it was done using the words of this or that ritual. An initiation is valid when it reaches in and touches the candidate deep within. Any of the Masonic rites are capable of doing that or not doing it. Problems for Lodges come not because they are practicing different rituals, but because they are not performing valid initiations.

But in reality, even with the claims of many that there is one craft ritual in the United States, over time these rituals have changed from jurisdiction to jurisdiction. Some variations in ritual are small and some large. It is far more likely that Masonic craft rituals are identical to each other within a jurisdiction than from jurisdiction to jurisdiction. It is because of the fact that jurisdictions are sovereign and independent that they have independently, and over time, made changes to their own ritual. These changes are often unique to their jurisdiction.

The 1700s and early 1800s were very creative times in Freemasonry. During the time when the Webb Ritual would become the ritual for the bulk of U.S. Masonry, there were many beautiful systems of Freemasonry created around the world. In many areas, multiple rituals worked side-by-side reflecting the rich nature of Masonic initiation. The enlightened do not view one ritual as better or superior to another, but only as a different path to reach the same destination.

The fact that Masonry in the United States does not utilize all of the different rituals, can be viewed as a missed opportunity for variety in lodge meetings, but really, in itself, that is only a minor inconvenience.

On the other hand, there is a misunderstanding, or a lack of understanding, concerning the nature of the Masonic Rites. This misunderstanding may exist because of the way that Freemasonry developed in the United States.

The two Masonic Rites which are dominant in the United States are the York Rite and the Scottish Rite. The Scottish Rite, or more correctly, the Ancient and Accepted Scottish Rite, is a 33 degree Masonic system. It was created in 1801 in Charleston,

South Carolina. The rituals used by this Rite come from older systems and rituals mainly from France. The other major Masonic rite in the U.S. is commonly known as the "York Rite" and concludes with the degree of Knight Templar. Sometimes also known as the "American Rite" it was hammered out around the same time that Webb was working on his craft rituals.

Albert Mackey used the term "American Rite" rather than "York Rite" as he felt the system was distinctly an American creation and to avoid confusion with systems and degrees of like name in England. Mackey was not successful in changing the official name of the rite and "York Rite" has become the popular and accepted name.

Because of the popularity of the two high degree Masonic systems that have survived in the U.S., and the desire for there to be only one craft ritual, a possibly unforeseen problem has developed. The problem when looked at from a Masonic ritualistic standpoint is that for something to be a Masonic Rite, it must begin in the craft lodge and then conclude at whatever final degree exists for that rite. The first degree of any Masonic rite must be the Entered Apprentice Degree

The situation for the United States, on first notice, is that we have two high grade Masonic rites that appear to begin *after* the Master Mason degree and then continue on to the completion of this system. Most Masons in the United States pay little attention to the degree progression and simply accept that the Masonic rites, the high-grade bodies, begin *after* the craft Lodge degrees. They appear separate and independent from craft Lodge Masonry.

Let's look at this situation. A good illustration for this discussion is an old Masonic print titled "The Steps of Freemasonry."

I find this piece of art very interesting. What I like about this particular piece of artwork is not that it portrays the actual nature of the Scottish Rite and the York Rite, but that it portrays how Freemasonry is worked from an organizational standpoint in the United States. I'd like to take a moment to examine this art and see exactly what is telling us as to how we view the Masonic rites.

The artwork is created along the lines of a pyramid with a base and then two sets of steps going up each side of the pyramid. If you look on the side labeled the Scottish Rite, it shows a step for each of the degrees and finally the degree of Sovereign Grand Inspector General, which is the 33rd and last degree. On the York Rite side, it also shows steps along with figures representing each of degrees of the York Rite concluding with its final step, the degree of Knight Templar. Also, if you look in the center area of the pyramid there is an arch, and inside of the arch there are a number of little figures which represent different organizations. This grouping of figures is identified as Allied Organizations. This collection is composed of organizations such as the Shrine, Grotto, the Eastern Star, and other Allied Organizations. These organizations are outside of the craft lodge, or outside of the actual rites of Freemasonry.

At the very bottom of the artwork you see three steps which provide the foundation for the whole pyramid. These three steps represent the craft lodge and the degrees of Entered Apprentice, Fellowcraft, and Master Mason. You see here a number of figures ascending up these steps. If you follow their directions, they go to the steps of the Scottish Rite or to the steps of the York Rite. The illusion and message that is given is that you have three separate set of steps available. There is the craft lodge steps, the steps of the Scottish Rite, and the steps of the York Rite.

The Allied Organizations are a bit higher up the steps and the suggestion is that once you have received your Master

The Steps of Freemasonry
SCOTTISH RITE
YORK RITE
ALLIED ORGANIZATIONS

Mason degree, you can apply to these bodies. The Shrine is set higher up on steps in this section as, for many years, in order to join the Shrine, you would either have to be a 32nd degree Scottish Rite Mason or a Knight Templar in the York Rite. This prerequisite has changed, and one needs only have received the Master Mason degree to become a Shriner today.

Now, if you take the Allied Organizations out of consideration and away from the image, you are left with the steps for the Scottish Rite, the York Rite, and the craft lodge degrees. The art seems to be suggesting that you have three separate entities. Since the craft lodge serves as the foundation piece, then once you have completed the steps of the craft lodge, you can then advance to the steps of the Scottish Rite or York Rite. The fact is that the Scottish Rite and the York Rite are both complete systems of Masonry with their own unique craft lodges. This artwork creates a misunderstanding as to the nature of a Masonic rite. Both the York Rite and the Scottish Rite begin their degree structure, or steps, in the Entered Apprentice degree. What is *not* delivered in this piece of art is that both the Scottish Rite as well as the York Rite have their own unique craft lodge rituals. All that is represented is *the* craft lodge. So, you don't realize that instead of two set of steps with a common foundation in the craft lodge, it should be two complete set of steps, each with their own individual craft lodge steps. Neither the Scottish Rite nor the York Rite begin their degrees *after* the Master Mason degree. The Scottish Rite and York Rite begin their systems in the own unique craft rituals.

In the New Orleans area, there are ten lodges working under the jurisdiction of the Grand Lodge of Louisiana which work in the Ancient and Accepted Scottish Rite craft Lodge ritual. This is the actual first three degrees of the Scottish Rite or otherwise known as the Scottish Rite blue lodge degrees.

As a side note, the Scottish Rite craft lodges in the New Orleans area have never been known by the term "Red Lodge." The term "Red Lodge" began and has been used in various places around the world to refer to Scottish Rite craft lodges, but not in New Orleans.

Regardless of how the poster "The Steps of Freemasonry" illustrates the nature of Freemasonry, The York Rite and the Scottish Rite each have their own unique foundational or craft lodge ritual. The foundational or craft lodge ritual for the York Rite is the ritual used in most all craft lodges in the United States. The foundational or craft lodge ritual for the Scottish Rite is limited, with rare exception, to the rituals used by the ten Lodges under the jurisdiction of the Grand Lodge of Louisiana. These ten Lodges comprise the 16th Masonic District of the Grand Lodge of Louisiana. In other areas of the world, however, the Scottish Rite craft ritual is one of the most popular of craft lodge rituals.

I believe the best way to understand the very easily to misunderstand nature of the American Masonic rites is to look at the very early days of masonry in the United States. Because of the early desire of the Masons in the new United States of America to have one Grand Lodge per state as well as one ritual per state, it created a situation which made it impossible to have approved multiple rituals worked in any of the jurisdictions.

When the 33 degree Ancient and Accepted Scottish Rite was created in 1801 in Charleston, South Carolina, a difficult situation already existed in that state. Without getting into a complex history of Masonry in England, there were two Grand Lodges in South Carolina which traced their roots to English Masonry but different styles of English Masonry.

I would recommend additional reading on the early history of English Freemasonry regarding the Ancients and the Moderns. These two Masonic philosophies resulted in two competing Grand Lodges in England, one commonly known as the Moderns and the other the Ancients. In 1813, they overcame their differences and joined together to create the United Grand Lodge of England.

In South Carolina in 1801, each of these English style Grand Lodges existed in the state. This presented problems to the rest of the U.S. Grand Lodges because of their desire to have only one Grand Lodge per state. On the surface, both of these Grand Lodges in South Carolina seemed perfectly regular and the desire for the balance of U.S. Freemasonry was for these two bodies to merge into one. The problem was that the members of these two Grand Lodges had a strong dislike of each other. They did not want to merge as each believed their own Grand Lodge possessed the correct Masonic philosophy.

Because of the problems created by these two Grand Lodges and their resistance to merge, it created an impossible situation for the Ancient and Accepted Scottish Rite when it was created in Charleston in 1801.

Simply put, the idea of a third body, the supreme council, controlling craft lodges in that state was unthinkable. The two Grand Lodges in South Carolina did eventually put aside their differences, merge, and become the Grand Lodge of South Carolina.

The Scottish Rite apparently traded their craft lodges for existence and only worked as an organization from the fourth degree onward. By doing this, the U.S. Masonic community could maintain their desire for one Grand Lodge and one ritual approved in each state.

In Louisiana, and while these ten Lodges working in the Scottish Rite ritual are under the jurisdiction of the Grand Lodge, the simple fact that more than one ritual existed created great problems in Louisiana Masonry in the mid-1800s.

The desire for one Grand Lodge and one ritual nearly tore Masonry apart in the state. This one Grand Lodge and one ritual per state concept also created misunderstanding about Masonic rites themselves.

As shown in the poster, the craft lodge became almost a separate entity rather than the foundational degrees of our Masonic rites.

A Masonic ritual is simply the vehicle used to deliver a Masonic initiation. If it were a play, it would be the script. A Masonic Rite is a particular type of ritual and all of the degrees that are associated with it. Throughout history, there have been many different Masonic rites and rituals. Each of the historic Masonic rituals and rites have their own unique beauty and manner of symbolic instruction.

In the early history of Masonry in the United States, we did have more Masonic rites than we do today. The Order of the Royal Secret, the French or Modern Rite, and the Egyptian Rite of Memphis are just a few of the rites once worked in the United States.

While the creative time in our Masonic history, when new Rites and rituals were commonplace, seems to have passed, who knows what tomorrow will bring? For all I know, a new wave of Masonic rites and rituals could be in our future. If there is one thing of which I'm certain, it is that no matter what we have today it will at some point change.

Notes:

1. Shepherd, Silas. "The Webb Ritual in the United States." *Masonic Enlightenment: The Philosophy, History and Wisdom of Freemasonry*. Ed. Michael R. Poll. New Orleans, LA: Cornerstone Book Publishers, 2006. pp 10-17.

With the Goal of Helping

I remember a good many years ago reading a story about someone trying to help others. It was one of these stories where you start off believing that it will take you in one direction, and then it ends up going in a completely different one, with a completely different moral lesson. The story is one of a young man who has a good heart and wants to help others. He would travel around doing good deeds for needy people. One day while going down a country road, he came upon a run down farmhouse. Clearly this was a poor family in need of help. He called on them and offered them assistance. When he entered the house, it was pretty much what he expected from a very poor family. The entire family looked thin and hungry, wearing only ragged clothes. There was very little furniture in the house and even less food. Then the man saw something completely unexpected. In a cabinet where he hoped to find food, he instead found many sacks of gold coins. This was not a poor family! In fact, this family was wealthier than anyone in the area. So why did they live as if they were poor?

The man was confused and frustrated. What a waste! Why would they live hungry and do without when the means to a prosperous life was right in front of them? The man tried to point out what they had at their fingertips and how different their life could be if they only made use of what they had stored away. The family completely rejected the man's advice. They said that they appreciated what he was trying to do, but that they could not use these coins and were trying to do the best that they could with their life. The family could not answer why they could not use the coins, and this only frustrated the man even more.

Angry at what he saw as an incredible lost opportunity, the man left the house telling the family that they were not only foolish but disrespectful to truly poor people. So outraged at the situation was the man that he simply could not let it go. To him, it was such a ridiculous situation that he made it his life's work to try to find a way to make these people see the error of their ways. He was going to find a way to stop making them live poor and make them use their own money to improve their lives. After a time, the young man's motivation moved from trying to help others to trying to get his own way. The family initially saw him as someone trying to help them, but then saw him as someone only set on harassment.

The family never did change their way of life, and the man never did find out why they refused to make their own lives better. For the rest of this man's life, he was frustrated by the actions of this family. Because he spent all of his time trying to find a way to make this one family change their mind, he helped no one else. Time and effort that could have been spent helping those truly in need was squandered on fighting a battle that he could not win. He went from living a generous, blessed life to living an empty, tormented one.

In Masonry, we often find lodges or other bodies in need of help. We should *always* do whatever we can to help spread Masonic education and be of service, whenever and however we can. But we must do so at the request of the lodge or body. Sometimes help is neither wanted nor appreciated. Yes, we may see the potential in a lodge very clearly. We may know that by doing this or that, they can greatly improve their entire lodge experience. But maybe they are happy and content with their current situation. Not everyone has the same goals or desires. We are all different. We have to know when offering help turns into pestering. Our time, attention, and efforts must be applied to where there is a *desire* to be helped.

The Masonic Legend of Hiram - Another Look

Around the world, there are many different types of Freemasonry. By that, I mean the rituals that are used and practiced. While the words and activities of the craft degrees in the different rites vary, sometimes quite a bit, there is one common thread that runs through all of the various rites and rituals — the legend of Hiram.

Now, before I write anything else, I have to throw in a disclaimer of sorts. Some time back I heard that a jurisdiction was thinking about removing the legend of Hiram from their ritual. As surprising as this information was, the reason behind their idea was even more remarkable. I was told that the reason for their wanting to remove this aspect of the ritual was because they could not establish if the legend of Hiram was a factual historical event. I was stunned. It's a *symbolic story* — a lesson. It is completely irrelevant if the story of Hiram is fact or fiction. Freemasonry is not teaching a history class. The story is used as a vehicle to deliver lessons of virtue and morality. The lessons that are taught are what is important, not the factual nature of the stories used to present the lessons. With that, we will continue.

The well published story of Hiram takes place at the time of the building of King Solomon's Temple. We are taught that a great many operative Masons worked on the construction of the Temple. These Masons were guided in their work by three Grand Masters: King Solomon, King Hiram of Tyre, and the lead architect, Hiram Abif.

At some point, the three Grand Masters realized that a number of the craftsmen were performing their duties at such a high level of skill that it entitled them to special recognition. These craftsmen would be elevated to Master craftsmen. Now, in today's Freemasonry, if we receive a degree, an office or position of importance, we're honored by that advancement. But in reality, it means very little outside of our Masonic life. Our Freemasonry is *Speculative* Freemasonry, and it is something we do *outside* of our family life and chosen livelihood. This was not the same with the old Operative Freemasons. Freemasonry was their livelihood. It was how they fed their family and paid their bills. Being advanced to the rank of Master was a big deal. Not only did it mean an elevation in their social status, it meant a considerable pay increase. This advancement was a very important event in their life.

When the news of the pending advancements was made known, we can assume that considerable excitement and interest developed. It is because of the importance of these advancements to the lives of those receiving them that some concern among the Grand Masters developed. It seemed reasonable to put into place some sort of security measure so that individuals of low moral character could not assume rank for which they were not entitled.

It was decided that a secret word would be given to all new Masters of the Craft so that they could prove their rank by possession of this word. As a further security measure, it was decided that this word would not be given out to anyone unless all three Grand Masters were present and agreed to the investiture.

The story goes on that three craftsmen obviously realized that they would likely *not* be elevated to a higher rank and were very unhappy about it. They wanted this advancement – badly. So much did they want this advancement that they hatched a plan to steal this "secret word," move to another area, and live their lives pretending to hold a rank that they did not earn.

They caught one of the Grand Masters alone and demanded that he tell them the secret word. Regardless of what they did, the Grand Master refused to give them this word. They became desperate. They made it clear to him that they were going to leave with either the word or him dead.

At this point, the Grand Master had a choice. He could give them what they wanted, or he could risk death. Clearly he took them seriously as his final words reflect acknowledgement of what he knew could happen.

And what happened next? Well, the ruffians made good on their threat, and they did kill him.

For a moment, stop and think about what happened. There is something that I was taught in childhood, and most likely, you have also been taught. It is that if I am ever in a situation where someone threatens my life in a robbery attempt, I should give them whatever they want. Why didn't he? I was taught that nothing I have on me is worth risking my life. Why didn't he just give them this word and then he could go on with his life?

The lesson of integrity is involved not because of a robbery attempt but because of an agreement that was made. This Grand Master agreed that he would not give the secret word to anyone unless certain conditions were met. Had these craftsmen attempted to simply rob him of some money, then it is reasonable that he would have freely exchanged whatever money he had on him for his life. But what these men wanted was something completely different. They demanded that he violate an agreement, his word.

Clearly the Grand Master recognized that he was not in control of their actions. He could not make them spare his life or do anything at all. Taking his life was something that they would either do or not do, and he had no control whatsoever over their actions. The only thing in which he had total control was *his* actions. They could take his life, but they could not take this word from him. He could only give it and that would be by *his* choice.

The Grand Master needed to determine what was of true value to him. He knew that we all live and die, but he also knew that *how* we live is up to us. To be robbed of some coins is no dishonor, but what of violating his word? What was that worth to him?

He did not agree to only give the word when certain conditions were met *unless* his life was threatened or only on the third Tuesday of the month if there was a full moon. He agreed to not give it unless these conditions were met. Period. If he gave the word to anyone and those conditions were not met then he would be violating his word. It didn't matter if they offered him money, threatened him, or anything else. He would either keep his word or break it.

In life we can gain or lose material things. Because of the twists and turns in life we can amass great wealth or lose everything we own. Many things can happen to us because we were either in the right place or the wrong place. But either we have integrity and honor, or we do not. We have it because it is our choice, and we lose it also by choice.

Material things can be taken away from us, and we might have no choice in the matter – but not our integrity. We are the only ones who have the power to give our integrity away.

The Grand Master knew that we all live and die. He also knew that all of the magnificent structures that he helped create would mean nothing if his moral foundation was made of sand – void of integrity and honor. These men had the power to take his life, but they were powerless to make him live a life without integrity.

This was the point of the story – to teach a life lesson of virtue and morality, not to simply provide a historical account. But we should not believe that the story ends there.

The nature of symbolism is layered and often requires second and third looks to find deeper meanings. Just because we *believe* that we are acting with honor or integrity does not mean that this is actually the case. Let me give you an example.

A story from New Orleans in the early 1800's comes to mind. There were two men who were standing outside the St. Louis Cathedral having a friendly conversation. The two men were facing each other. One of the men felt a bit uncomfortable in his position and moved just a bit to the left to reposition himself.

When the man moved over, the other man winced in pain and looked shocked. In a sharp tone he demanded that the man return to his original position. The man who moved had no idea of what the other man was speaking, but he did not like his tone of voice.

What neither man realized or considered was that the man who moved was considerably taller than the other man. In the position he was standing, he (unknown to either man) was standing right in a place where he was blocking the sun. When he moved a bit over, the sunlight hit the shorter man right in the eyes causing his painful reaction.

Neither man was of a mind to explain himself or ask too many questions of the other. Hot tempers took over and the friendly conversation was replaced by a very heated, nonsensical argument. And then it happened ... one man exclaimed that his "honor" had become compromised and "integrity" demanded satisfaction.

He challenged the other man to a duel.

It was fortunate that neither man died in the duel, but one of them was shot in the arm. For the rest of his life, he lived with a useless arm as the result of the injury suffered in that duel. And for what? Honor? Integrity? One man moved a bit, and the other man had sun in his eyes. For that you shoot at each other?

What these men mistook for honor and integrity was pride, arrogance, and vanity. These vices were disguised as, or mistaken for, virtues.

There was no loss of honor in what happened and integrity demanded nothing in the way of a duel. We must live our lives with honor and integrity. But we must know what is a virtue and what is a vice disguised as virtue. It's not always as clear as we think.

There will be times when we find it most difficult to understand or live up to our teachings. But, as we are so often told, it is the journey that is most important, not the final goal.

The Scottish Rite Double Headed Eagle (Phoenix?)

At the very start, I'd like to confess that this paper is probably a lot more opinion than provable fact. It has to do with what might be the most recognizable symbol of the Scottish Rite – the Double-Headed Eagle.

For many the symbol is just accepted for what it is – an eagle with two heads. But for those more esoterically inclined Scottish Rite Masons, there seems to be a desire to look more into that symbol. They want to know what it means, why it was selected, and if there is more to it than meets the eye.

We can really take the question of the Double-Headed Eagle in several directions. We can look at it by what is provable, by what we think, or a combination of both. Let's start with the idea that maybe something right in front of us can be more than what we may initially believe. Let's also say that *truth* may have levels to it. Let me give you an example.

I grew up on an army base on the outskirts of New Orleans. My father was a career military man. I remember as a boy going shopping on Canal Street with my family and then returning home by way of a back shortcut. Where we lived was right up against the Mississippi River. Most of the way home was residential, but there was one area that we would pass that was about four blocks of open area. A section was fenced in with a large, old wooden structure towards the back, looking something like a massive barn.

As a child, I had no idea what this strange looking place might be. In the fenced in area, there was always a number of cows grazing on the grass. I remember coming home one day and asking my mother about this strange place. She almost brushed off the question and simply answered me, "Oh, that's just the abattoir."

I remember asking her, "What's that?" She told me that that's where they kept all the cows – made sense. I didn't give the place much more thought until years later when during a French class I learned that *abattoir* was a French word for *slaughterhouse*.

I remember asking my mother about both the word and the place that she called the abattoir. She told me that she didn't want to exactly tell me what that place was as she felt I was too young to deal with it, but she also didn't want to lie to me. Her solution was to do to me as her mother had done to her, and that was to use French as the *adult language* when they did not want the children to know exactly what they were talking about. What I knew and understood was based on my own limitations. As I grew in knowledge, my understanding of what that place actually was grew as well.

Freemasonry is very clear with the fact that it employs symbolism in its manner of education. If we see any symbol as being limited to only one meaning or interpretation, then we may be missing much from that symbol. Our goal is to make the individual "better" through education and, of course, *better* is subjective. And, how we become *bette*r depends on us.

We are not all the same. There is no one size fits all. We all come with our own levels of desires, awareness, and interest. For a symbol to be of most value, it would need to be useful to those with different needs or goals. How one sees or understands a symbol may well be completely different then how another sees it. And this does not mean that either is correct or incorrect. We all take from symbols what we want and need.

I know that there are Masonic books out there that take something of a hard line on Masonic symbols. Some feel that the symbols of Freemasonry are limited to *only* what we are told that they mean. I strongly disagree with this way of thinking. I believe that a symbol can also have very private meanings that speak only to a few.

The value of a symbol is not determined by the number of individuals who understand it. It is also possible for a symbol to be understood as one thing for many years and then be taken over by others to mean something completely different. Look at the Swastika. This was a beautiful and meaningful symbol used by a number of cultures long before the Nazis existed. Did the Nazis destroy this symbol? Well, they certainly damaged it and perverted the original meaning. Maybe with enough time the original beauty of the symbol can be recognized. How much time will be needed before that can take place I can't say.

This brings us to the Double-Headed Eagle. What does it mean? What *did* it mean? And what *can* it mean?

Let's try to take a look at these questions. First, we must understand the environment of our subject. The Double-Headed Eagle is currently the most noted symbol of the thirty-three degree Ancient and Accepted Scottish Rite. This system of Freemasonry was created in 1801 in Charleston, South Carolina.

But clearly what we know as the "Double-Headed Eagle" was employed by many earlier groups, royal houses, and Masonic Orders. So, why was the Double-Headed Eagle adopted as the symbol of the Ancient and Accepted Scottish Rite?

Well, it *was* a prominent symbol for the older Order of the Royal Secret, so maybe it was intended to be a carryover, or a tie to that system. We also have to think about the Grand Constitutions of 1786. These were the documents claimed to be authorized or approved by Frederick the Great giving legitimacy to this new Scottish Rite system. Interestingly enough, the Double-Headed Eagle was the Royal Symbol for Frederick.

While serious Masonic historians today discount the Grand Constitutions of 1786 as a forgery, the Double-Headed Eagle was certainly *not* a creation of the early Charleston Council nor anyone associated with them. Selecting this symbol for the early Charleston Supreme Council does, however, make perfect sense. It ties this new system to the old system and also brings together the Grand Constitutions of 1786 and Frederick the Great – and all through the Double-Headed Eagle.

It's not possible to enter the minds of the members of the early Charleston Council to know their knowledge (or opinion) of this particular symbol. I have also never seen anything explaining *exactly* why they chose this particular symbol for this new system. It is possible that for the early Charleston Council, no deeper meaning for this symbol existed. But this is only a theory without any supporting evidence.

But it does lead us to the next question in the chain of evidence. Why did the Order of the Royal Secret use the Double-Headed Eagle? It's also a dead end for me. I don't have this answer either. Just like the early Charleston Supreme Council, I've seen no records explaining exactly why the symbol was used by them.

Maybe we should turn in another direction and look at another question that is often asked about the symbol. The question is a very straightforward one. Is the bird in that symbol actually an eagle, or could it be a Phoenix?

The Phoenix is an ancient bird symbol. The legend goes that this bird would live for hundreds of years and then towards the end of its life would settle down, become inactive, and then burst into flames in what seemed to be a fiery death. But instead of disintegrating into ashes, the Phoenix would be reborn out of the flames. This cycle of life, bursting into flames, and then being reborn out of the flames would continue possibly indefinitely.

Some claim that the Phoenix represents the pure philosophy that ties Freemasonry to the ancient mystery schools. This philosophy lives forever and whenever human nature degrades it to a level that it is no longer useful it goes through this purging cycle, just as the Phoenix, to be reborn anew.

I believe that one of the great problems that we as humans have is assuming things. If we don't have a clear and quick answer to something, we sometimes assume an answer. A good example of this is the 1979 movie titled "Being There" with Peter Sellers. In this movie Sellers portrays a simpleminded, middle-aged man who works as a gardener for a wealthy, elderly man. When the elderly man passes away, the simpleminded gardener, who was a ward of the elderly man, does not comprehend the situation, what he should do, or what is expected of him. He lived in this home since childhood and is bewildered at the changes in his routine. Because the gardener was always allowed to take and wear expensive clothing from the attic, characters in the movie mistook him for a wealthy businessman following a mishap.

The gardener's simple manner of speech and demeanor are mistaken for great wisdom. They extend to him every privilege and treat him with great respect. They *assume* that something great was there when, in fact, nothing at all was there.

Sometimes we treat those who employ symbols in the same manner. Someone may open a store and use an ancient, very meaningful symbol in association with their business. It is possible that they fully understand the meaning of the symbol, and it is also possible that they understand nothing of it and only like the look of the design as a logo.

We should not assume before we completely understand. I can't tell you what was in the minds of the early Charleston Members, nor with the early Members of the Order of the Royal Secret, nor any of the older groups that used it. I can't tell you what they knew or believed. I don't know if they saw the Double-Headed Eagle as an eagle with two heads, a Phoenix with two heads, or a Phoenix disguised as an eagle. I also don't know if they knew why it had two heads.

I can only tell you that this symbol is, among other things, an ancient alchemical symbol representing rebirth, life, growth, and much more depending on the eyes and path of the viewer.

I can tell you that students of the Scottish Rite can benefit by taking second, third, and fourth looks at this symbol.

In my opinion, it does not matter, at all, if the ones who placed this symbol into the Scottish Rite possessed full knowledge of its meaning, or had no knowledge at all of any possible meaning. All that matters is that it is here, and it is worth serious study by those who seek more out of the Scottish Rite.

Those who believe there is nothing more to study or research are simply mistaken. In my opinion, the Double-Headed Phoenix, may well be under the guise of an eagle, and that's OK. Maybe the time is now to take a good look at this symbol, see how it relates to the state of affairs in Masonry today, and put this important symbol to use.

Right now, being reborn better than ever, sounds pretty good to me.

The Tactics of the Anti-Masons

Some years back a Mason told me of an encounter that he had with an anti-Mason. He was not a new Mason, but he was shocked at the encounter. He had difficulty understanding the logic of the anti-Mason. He told me that he had known the man for many years and considered him a friend, but the subject of Freemasonry had never come up in any of their conversations. When the man learned that he was a Freemason, his entire attitude towards him changed. He then began making charges that the Mason *knew* were not correct, but because he was not a student of Masonic history nor was he well read in its philosophy, he was not able to properly defend Masonry from the many charges that the man made. He said it was a helpless feeling to hear what he knew were false charges being made but being unable to properly mount any sort of defense.

The fact is that anti-Masonry has existed for about as long as Freemasonry has existed. There is a thought that for the world to be in proper balance everything must have an equal opposite. For there to be light there must be dark, if there is good there must also be bad and so on. If Freemasonry is the pure philosophy that is represented to be, then we must understand that it must have an opposite.

Freemasonry must be challenged and forced to defend itself from the other end of the spectrum if it is to remain a pure philosophy. If this thought is correct, then anti-Masonry is not a phenomena in need of being crushed out. Anti-Masonry is very much needed to provide balance to the Masonic philosophy and to remain a constant test to it so that it does not diminish in value.

But understanding the greater reasons of why anti-Masonry may exist is not very helpful if anti-Masons are making actual attacks on Freemasonry or Freemasons themselves. The fact is that we must know Freemasonry if we are to defend it. If all we do is attend business meetings, listen to minutes, visit with friends and drink coffee, then it is no wonder we won't be able to defend Masonry when falsehoods are written or spoken.

In his paper, *The Rise and Development of Anti-Masonry in America 1737- 1826,* [1] J. Hugo Tatsch tells us of a very disturbing early account of anti-Masonry. He writes of a con-man who tricked people into joining what he said was Freemasonry only to put them through ridiculous and humiliating situations for personal entertainment. The bogus rituals ended deadly when one candidate was set on fire and died a painful death several days later. Because the man represented himself *as Freemasonry,* actual Freemasonry was painted with his brush.

From the way things seem to me, there are three general categories of anti-Masonry. One is fanatic anti-Masonry where individuals choose to believe pretty much anything at all about Masonry simply because someone, usually a man representing himself as a man of the cloth, tells them that nonsense is fact. Their belief of terrible things about Masonry becomes almost interwoven into their religious faith.

Another form of anti-Masonry is business anti-Masonry. Some individuals advance all sorts of anti-Masonic activity and teachings, even some in the guise of religion, but the end is always to sell things for personal profit. Since they make a good living off anti-Masonry, they are hardly ready to change their tune.

The third form of anti-Masonry is a bit more complicated. It is when individuals will start *what they claim to be* Masonic Lodges, identify themselves *to be* Masonic Lodges, then con those who know no better into joining them. They make their living off of *pretending* to be Masonry, but offer nothing in the way of Masonry to those who join them. The general public, often knowing little to nothing of Masonry, believe them to be true Masonry, recognize what they did as a con, and blame Freemasonry itself. The whole of Masonry suffers.

Let's look deeper at these situations.

Back in 1980s, I had two first-hand accounts of what could be called fanatical anti-Masonry. I remember there was a woman who was a yoga instructor and my mother was a student of hers. This instructor and my mother became friends, and I remember the instructor coming over to the house often to visit.

At some point thereafter, the yoga instructor joined a church which felt that yoga was an abomination. This church also taught that anyone who belonged to Freemasonry was not only a sinner, but also not a Christian — no matter what they believed. Now, I didn't know anything about this, and one day I came into the house to find both of them talking. The woman was telling my mother how she was giving up teaching yoga and the reasons for it. As they were talking, the woman looked up and saw my Masonic ring. Without hardly missing a beat, she looked me right in the eyes and said, "You don't believe in God." I was caught off guard, surprised, and not sure of exactly what to say to the woman. I simply told her that I did believe in God. She immediately told me that I was wrong. She said that she knew that I did not. I was young at the time and not completely prepared to deal with something that seems so absurd to me. I couldn't understand how she could believe that she had any idea as to what was in my heart. I asked her how she could believe such a thing about someone she didn't really know. She said that her minister told her. I was even more shocked and still not sure that I was hearing her correctly. I pointed out that this was not a better answer, as her minister had never laid eyes on me. She told me that her minister told her that anyone who does not belong to her church does not believe in God. I was stunned at the total illogic of such an answer. I attributed the problem to her personally and assumed that she must be an irrational person (I thought she was nuts). I dismissed the event as just nonsense from a strange woman.

About six months to a year later a second incident happened. I was working at the time in downtown New Orleans and parking in that area was very expensive. We had a convenient public transportation system, and I would take the bus to work every day. I would come home every evening about the same time. As I was walking home, I would pass a neighbor's house who lived down the street from me. Most days I would see him sitting out in a lawn chair reading his Bible. I didn't really think that much of it. I would normally waive at him and ask how he was doing. We didn't get into any long conversations, but the greetings were always friendly. One day we were exchanging a few words, and he noticed that I was wearing a Masonic ring. His attitude changed a bit, and he asked if I was a Freemason. I told him yes. He then told me that I probably didn't know that this was an evil organization. He said that he had proof that would confirm what he said. He asked if I would wait for a minute, and he would get me this "proof." I knew that he was wrong, but I was not in a mood to debate him so I just told him "No, thanks" dismissed the conversation, and went home.

For about a month or so after, every time that neighbor saw me he would ask if I could give him a few moments so that he could show me the "proof" that he had on Masonry. He said that he had the documents that would show without question that Freemasonry was Satanic. He said that he cared about me and didn't want me to continue "sinning" by being a member. I normally just waved at him and told him that I didn't have time. Well, one Friday he caught me in the right mood, and I told him that I would take a look at what he had. He went inside and came back with a briefcase. The briefcase was filled with a large number of photocopies of various documents. He said that this was the proof that Freemasonry is evil. I told him that this was far too many documents to review at that moment, and I asked him if I could take them home with me for the weekend so that

I could look at them. He told me that this was fine, and I went home to look over the material.

When I started looking through the documents in the briefcase, I saw that they was all photocopies from various anti-Masonic books and leaflets. All the copies showed various quotes which seemed to be from Masons. Each of the quotes looked to be properly cited. I happen to have a fairly good Masonic library, and I had a copy of each of the books from where the quotes were taken. Invariably, each and every quote that was cited was either out of context, misquoted, or completely made up. I remember one quote that was given from a Grand Master giving a speech, and the quote was, "Masonry is evil, it is satanic." I looked in the book from where the speech was transcribed and what the Grand Master actually said was, "I would be telling a lie if I said that Masonry is evil, it is satanic." So I sat down and for each and every quote that he gave, I provided the correction from the original source. I guess that I was naïve because I thought that by providing him with all the corrections, he would change his view of Freemasonry. I fully expected to sit down with him, show him the corrections and for him to say, "Gee, I guess I was wrong about Freemasonry."

Well, I went back to the man's house and sat down with him. I showed him each one of the pieces of his evidence and how each one of them did not truly say what it was claimed that they did say. There was no debate in the matter; the proof that he said he was going to show me simply did not exist. When I finished, he didn't say anything; he just sat there. I finally said, "Do you see that the proof you said you were going to show me does not exist?" The man looked me right in the eyes and said, "No, I don't see that at all. Jesus is my proof." I was completely baffled. I grew up as a Christian, but not once had I have been taught that Jesus supported falsehoods. He had created a situation where he knowingly and willingly accepted lies and his only defense was a professed belief that Jesus would agree with supporting falsehoods. I didn't know what to say, so I left.

Someone who I consider to be a religious fanatic is *not* one who simply holds strongly to a religious belief. The very nature of religion means that it goes outside of the realm of scientific proof. A religious fanatic is one who will take *an unsanctioned* detail of their religion and then deny truth itself in order to hold onto that religious modification. An example would be an anti-Mason who believes various things about Freemasonry as my former neighbor did. They will hold onto these misconceptions *as* a religious belief, even when they are proven incorrect. Another example would be the friend of my mother who claimed to *know the heart* of a stranger. She claimed to *know* the private beliefs of a stranger simply on the suggestion of her minister. The fanatical aspects of these people had *nothing to do* with their belief in a Supreme Being; it had to do with the *judgments* they freely made about other human beings.

There is another type of anti-Masonry that began in the 1990s that created a good bit of excitement in U.S. Masonry. I don't really know if this particular anti-Masonic movement was *always* the way it evolved into, or if it was born one way and then evolved in a different direction. In the late 80s and early 90s there was unrest in the religious organization known as the Southern Baptist Convention. A small group of members began an organized attack on Freemasonry. Their claim was that Freemasonry was incompatible with Christianity. Their support for this claim was exactly the same as the "proof" displayed by my former neighbor – meaning, out of context quotes, misquotes, and outright created quotes. The problem for many Masons was that they did not have readily available Masonic reference books and were unable to properly counter the charges made against them.

It was around this time that a Masonic friend of mine, Arturo de Hoyos, co-authored a book with S. Brent Morris titled, *Is it True What They Say About Freemasonry*? Initially, I was critical of this book as I felt it was improper for Freemasons, *or Freemasonry,* to dignify such irrational attacks. I felt that their talents were better suited in other areas of research. I didn't feel it *fitting* for them to attempt to change the mind of those who did not want their minds changed. *I was wrong.* I considered this movement a totally fanatical movement. I failed to realize, *at the beginning,* that business played a part in this particular anti-Masonic movement.

The young internet was used successfully by these anti-Masons in order to spread their Masonic propaganda. Mixed in with their falsehoods was a cleverly disguised sales campaign. We must understand that the libraries possessed by most Masons consist of, at most, a few general Masonic encyclopedias. Most Masons were unable to properly defend and expose the so-called "proof" of these anti-Masons for what it was.

The documents containing misquotes, out of context quotes, and outright made up quotes made impressive sounding and very believable evidence to those who knew little of Freemasonry. It was not long before books were written *by* these anti-Masons containing this false information. Because of their religious sounding delivery method and persistence of these anti-Masonic leaders, these books did become popular and before long successful anti-Masonic businesses were created.

Grand Lodges had long been lax in maintaining things such as copyrights on their monitors and other printed material. Most Grand Lodges were also more concerned with replenishing dwindling membership than fighting possibly difficult copyright battles with anti-Masons. The result was that monitors and other printed material were stolen by anti-Masons and reprinted by them to be sold on their websites. These anti-Masons found a good business in selling falsehoods. Believable arguments were made, and it was an attractive sales technique. It was successful.

Around this same time, CompuServe was a popular internet service provider. CompuServe offered community forums on a very wide variety of interests. For those discovering the young internet, the CompuServe forums were extremely interesting and popular. It was here that one of the very early Masonic forums was created – the CompuServe Masonry Forum. There were also several religion forums on CompuServe and these were soon discovered by anti-Masons. The anti-Masons had made several attempts to post their propaganda on the CompuServe Masonry Forum itself, but they were quickly booted off. They were, however, able to find a home on several of the CompuServe religious forums, and the campaign of lies began. Of course, along with that was near not stop reference to where so-called "true Christians" could buy "proof" of the anti-Masonic charges and support "God's" work. This was indeed a cleverly disguised moneymaking scheme that was successful for a number of years.

I personally learned how wrong I was about the work of Brothers de Hoyos and Morris when I began taking part in what would become the "CompuServe Anti-Masonic Debates." These were a series of debates, *or nasty arguments,* taking place mostly on the various CompuServe religion forums. The anti-Masons would make charges and knowledgeable Masons would refute the charges. The anti-Masons would then pivot to make new charges only to then go back to their initial charge *as if it had never been answered.* It was all tactics and games.

These so-called anti-Masons were really clever salesmen who were skilled in the bait and switch technique. Masons taking part in the defense of Freemasonry were put through extraordinarily difficult and frustrating times with having to answer the same question, over and over again. What became clear very quickly was that there was no changing the minds of the ones making the charges. They were fixed in their opinion, and nothing would change it.

The ones who could be changed and influenced by the truth, were often the silent readers who had little to no knowledge of Freemasonry. Many of the ones who had only read the various posts and never stepped out of the shadows had no idea as to what was, or was not, true. They had no preconceived ideas of Freemasonry itself and had no reason to doubt, initially, either the anti-Masons or the Masons. These individuals were Christian and because of the nature of the charges made by the anti-Masons they were interested in the claims and did purchase material from them because of the subject matter.

Because of the work of the Masonic researchers who took part in these debates, many honest and objective Christians came to see the lies being peddled by these anti-Masonic businessmen. I realized that if Masons ignored these anti-Masonic charges, it would harm the Masonic organization itself due to the persuasive nature of the anti-Masonic sales techniques.

But what is the real difference between a religious fanatic and a religious businessman intent on selling a religious belief? While there may be psychological or philosophical differences between the mindsets, the reality is that neither has a desire to allow *facts* to change their position. You cannot change the mind of someone who *wants* to believe something. It is only when someone is open to the truth, that facts have any importance.

One of the great benefits of these CompuServe anti-Masonic debates was a particular website that came out as a result of these debates. The website was a creation of Worshipful Brother Ed King of Maine, and is titled "Anti-Masonry: Points of View." (http://www.masonicinfo.com) This website is an absolute gold mine of information on anti-Masons, their techniques and the charges that are commonly made by them. It is an extremely valuable website for obtaining verifiable information and clearing up the smoke and mud thrown by the anti-Masons.

While the anti-Masonic frenzy of the 90's has generally past, a number of these anti-Masonic businessmen still exist and still do con many individuals.

There is a third form of anti-Masonry that I believe needs to be mentioned. This form of activity is more closely tied to the anti-Masonic businessmen than the fanatic anti-Masons in that making money seems to be their main goal. This form of anti-Masonry is where businessmen set up, what appears to be, a Masonic Grand Lodge with the goal of creating Masons. Of course these bodies are created with no authority whatsoever and are the textbook definition of irregular. The main goal of most of these self-created grand lodges is to make money for the few at the very top, and give nothing in the way of Masonry to the members.

Prince Hall Masonry uses a term that I believe is very appropriate for these types of Masonic *businesses*. Their term is "bogus Masonry." The term "bogus Masonry" very nicely applies to these self-created bodies which are more on the lines of moneymaking schemes. I've long felt that there is a need for a third branch in the Masonic tree. What I see as the three branches are: regular Masonry, irregular Masonry, and bogus Masonry. Regular Freemasonry is simply legitimate Freemasonry. It is the Masonry that is recognized and conducts itself as regular. Irregular Masonry is Masonry that has some problem with its organization or ritual. It is not viewed by regular Freemasonry as regular. But bogus Masonry is different from irregular Masonry in that many times irregular Masonic bodies do seem to attempt to, at least, practice regular Freemasonry. The problem with irregular Masonry is that many times they just do not have legitimate origins. Bogus Masonry is more often than not simply moneymaking schemes by con-men who attempt to personally profit off of Freemasonry's reputation.

Some years back I heard of a classic example of bogus Masonry and I believe this example needs to be retold to show the danger to regular Freemasonry. In this case, several con-men decided to create their own Grand Lodge in an African-American community. They paid close attention to what was going on in the community. They learned of a man who had recently been diagnosed with terminal cancer. He was given only a few months to live. This was a hard-working man with a family. The news of his illness was especially hard on him, not only because of the fact of the illness, but because he was not at all a wealthy man who did not know how his family would survive without him.

One evening a knock came on the door. Several men had come calling identifying themselves as "the Freemasons." They told the man and his wife that they had learned of his unfortunate illness and situation. They said that they may be able to help. They said that if this man would join the Freemasons they would assure that he would have a Masonic funeral and burial *at no expense* to the family. They said that they would also provide several bags of groceries to the man's widow each week and see to it that his children would remain in school until they are graduated or were of age. They said that the fee to join the Masons was $200. They left the man and his wife to think about the offer and said that they would return in a few days.

The man and his wife had heard of Freemasonry and had heard that it was an honorable organization. But $200 was about all they had in savings. Realizing that this money would not even pay for the funeral, they felt that joining would be a wise way to invest the money for the future of the family. They decided that it would be best for him to join. The men returned a few days later, were given the $200 and the sick man was given a dues card and told that he was now a member of the Freemasons.

They left. Nothing more was heard from them.

The man passed away, and, of course, these con-men were nowhere to be found. Months after the man passed away his widow saw one of the men on the street. She approached him in anger and desperation. She wanted to know why they had not come back. She said her husband passed away, and they did *nothing at all*. She reminded him of all that they had promised prior to her husband's joining.

The man said that there must be a misunderstanding. He said that they did fulfill everything as promised. He said that her husband gave them $200 and that this was the "Master Mason's Package." He said for that they said a prayer in Lodge for the man and recorded his name in their list of "honored members." He said that what she was talking about was the "33rd Degree Package." He said that this package would have cost $5,000. Of course, the woman realized that she had been tricked by this thief.

While she realized this man's nature, she did not realize that he was only *pretending* to be a Mason. From that day on *anyone* who identified himself as a Freemason was viewed by her and everyone she could tell as a thief and a con-man. This group of bogus Masons, thieves and con-men, not only deeply damaged and hurt this family, but the whole of Freemasonry with their deception.

This is why I believe that special notice should be taken of this particular brand of anti-Masonry. The damage it does to individuals, the community, and Freemasonry itself cannot be minimized. It must be exposed and by every legal measure crushed out.

No matter what we like, dislike, want, or reject, anti-Masonry has been a thorn in the side of Freemasonry for nearly as long as it has existed. The limitations of this paper do not allow for all accounts of anti-Masonry around the world. Religious fanatics and con-men have *not* been the only anti-Masons. Political dictators as well as anyone seeking to destroy freedom have been strongly opposed to Freemasonry. Even a few world and religious leaders, such as Pope Leo 13th and U.S. President John Adams have been famous anti-Masons. Albert Pike has long been a target of anti-Masons due to his often difficult to understand, or open to interpretation, language. But it is not just Pike's language that has been a point of confusion or attack. Many Masonic words and phrases are simply archaic and odd sounding to the ear. They are ripe for attack by those wishing to make something out of nothing.

The early 1900's were a time of more than a few notable Masonic con-men including Matthew McBlain Thomson and his notorious American Masonic Federation and the almost comical "TK and his Great Work," whose real name was John E. Richardson.

Anti-Masons have also been capable of serious damage to Freemasonry. Space does not permit a close examination of the

William Morgan Affair, but the effects of this anti-Masonic attack nearly destroyed the whole of Masonry in the New England states and even more areas of the US in the 1820's, and for a good 20 or so years later. For an excellent account of this event, see Stephen Dafoe's, *Morgan: The Scandal That Shook Freemasonry.* [3]

But, with all that anti-Masonry has done, or tried to do, Freemasonry still exists. We are stronger because of the trials and tribulations of these attacks. I imagine that if anti-Masonry did not exist, Freemasonry could become complacent and become disconnected from its goals and philosophy. So we must learn to live with the dark in order to enjoy the light.

Notes:

1. Tatsch, J. Hugo. "The Rise and Development of Anti-Masonry in America 1737- 1826." *Masonic Enlightenment: The Philosophy, History and Wisdom of Freemasonry.* Ed. Michael R. Poll. New Orleans, LA: Cornerstone Book Publishers, 2006. pp 126-138.

2. de Hoyos, Arturo and Morris, S. Brent. *Is it True What They Say About Freemasonry?* Silver Spring, Md. M.S.A., 1994.

3. Dafoe, Stephen. *Morgan: The Scandal That Shook Freemasonry.* New Orleans, LA: Cornerstone Book Publishers, 2006.

The Ritual Trap

I have long believed that within our ritual is the core of our Masonic teachings. The rituals are much more than just a play designed to entertain the membership. In fact, when the ritual is degraded to the point that it is viewed as entertainment by the membership, our Masonic initiation is also degraded to the point that it becomes meaningless. There are few things more disgraceful than members of a Lodge entertaining themselves at the expense of a candidate. Not only is the opportunity for meaningful initiation lost to the candidate, but the Lodge is reduced to a nonsensical fraternity club. Our candidates, the Lodge, and our rituals deserved more.

Since learning aspects of the ritual in our catechism is required by all who join,[1] all Masons have some familiarity with our ritual. Of course, learning the catechism required to advance through the degrees does not make one a ritualist. But learning the ritual does give the opportunity to spot a ritualist. Those with a knack for ritual can be easily identified with how they handle the memorization of the catechism. But what exactly is the role of a ritualist in the Lodge? How we identify and define the role of the ritualist in the Lodge plays a part in the nature of the Lodge itself. If the role of the ritualist is misunderstood then this can cause problems for the Lodge if the Lodge desires to go in one direction only to find the ritualist going in another direction. Let me explain.

The Lodge's view of our Masonic ritual falls into three main categories. This would be how the Lodge members view the importance and meaning of the ritual. One group are those who do not care about good ritual or what the ritual means; another group are those who care about good ritual, but believe that the meaning of the ritual is not very important; and the final group are those who do care about good ritual and what the ritual means or teaches us.

When we visit a Lodge, its nature or personality can often be determined rather quickly. Most successful Lodges will have members who, prior to the Lodge meeting, will seem in good humor, and enjoyable conversations will be taking place between the brothers, maybe over a meal. This atmosphere of enjoyment is necessary for any Lodge wishing to survive, but it itself, is not a guarantee of success. It doesn't matter if the Lodge is formal in nature, sometimes called Traditional Observance, or if the Lodge is casual and truly little more than a social club. A successful Lodge can be one that is defined in nature by the membership and what they desire. But once the time comes for the Lodge meeting to start, we have the opportunity to see the true nature of the Lodge.

The first thing that is noticed is how the officers are dressed and act in their stations. They may be dressed up, maybe not tuxes, but in the coat and tie or at the very least nice slacks and shirts. These officers will assume their stations with an air of responsibility and confidence. When the meeting starts, they will deliver their parts of the ritual for the opening letter perfect or near letter perfect. They will act dignified in these stations with all present fully aware that what is taking place is significant and meaningful. This will be a Lodge that is taken seriously. Of course, this type of Lodge is not the only type of Lodge that can be successful. We do find lodges where the officers come to their stations in jeans are other casual attire. They often joke and laugh just prior to the opening and assume the stations in a casual manner. The opening ritual is often filled with errors and prompting is needed for many to most of the officers. It is clear that learning the ritual is not that important to them and not the main reason why they are in the Lodge.

Mind you, we are only talking about successful Lodges. A failing Lodge may operate exactly the same, but that is a different story. There are successful casual Lodges, who meet pretty much as a social club with not much more expected or desired from or by the members.

In my experience, a common thread in all casual or social club lodges is the apparent disregard that they have for learning the ritual. The ritual is just something that needs to be muddled through in order to open the meeting. It plays no other role in the Lodge function and could easily be done away with in this type of Lodge setting.

On the other end of the spectrum is the Lodge where the ritual is viewed as the cornerstone of the Lodge. The ritual is not only learned by the officers, but its meaning is taught to all the membership in classes during Lodge meetings. It is realized, in these Lodges, that within the ritual is symbolic teachings of the Lodge and these teachings are expounded to the membership.

The difference in nature of these two types of Lodges is that one serves only as a social club and the other to teach the lessons of Freemasonry. In my experience, both types of Lodges can be successful depending on what the membership wants. Each type of Lodge must understand themselves, the type of Lodge that they have, and a recognition that this is what they want out of their Masonic experience.

What I have found is that problems can come with the third type of Lodge. This would be the Lodge that professes that the ritual is important but does not teach either the meaning of the ritual, nor insist that the officers of the Lodge be proficient in the ritual. This type of Lodge does not truly acknowledge its own nature nor understand or accept what is necessary to be something else.

As with everything in life, we have choices in Freemasonry. We can choose whatever path we want. We can participate in whatever type of Masonry we want. We can also lie to ourselves. We can go down a path that is clearly painted green and tell the whole world, and ourselves as well, that it is painted blue. We have that right and that ability.

There is nothing in the world wrong with belonging to a Lodge that is little more than a social club. Many social club Lodges do wonderful charitable work. They are made up of members who would, if needed, give you the shirt off their back. They are good men. However, they do not take advantage of the deeper lessons in Freemasonry. These lodges do not study the ritual or use it as part of their regular education program of self-improvement. They simply go to Lodge, enjoy a meal, talk with their friends, read bills during the meeting, and discuss plans for this or that program. There is nothing wrong with that, but the simple truth is that this was not the original plan or goal of Freemasonry. It is a stripped-down modification of the original design. Those who recognize this, and accept it, can have a successful Lodge of this nature. They have selected a path to travel and are satisfied with it.

The Lodges that teach Masonic education, do the work that Freemasonry was designed to do, have also selected a path. They understand what they want to do, what they need to do to achieve it, and do the work necessary to achieve their goals of self-improvement.

Both of these types of Lodges have picked a lane, they have selected a path to travel. They both can be successful as long as they understand what they are and what they are not. They can work well as long as they stay in their lane and continue on their chosen path.

It is that third group of Lodges that have the most trouble. These are the ones who do not understand what or who they are. They don't understand what is necessary for them to do nor do they properly understand the direction they wish to take. They very often fall into a ritual trap that results in internal frustration and an inability to be what they want no matter how hard they seem to work.

The third type of Lodge falls into the trap of believing all is well, when all is far from well. I believe that the problem comes from a false belief about the ritual as well as the role that members play in the leadership of the Lodge. In the *Old Charges of a Mason*, there is an interesting line which reads, "no Master or Warden is chosen by seniority, but for his merit." What does *merit* mean? What is considered merit if not seniority? Does it mean leadership abilities? Sure, sounds like it does. So then, should we consider someone good in business to be excellent material for a Lodge officer? Maybe, maybe not.

In Operative Masonry, the leaders were chosen by those who were considered the most skilled craftsmen. The ones who were best able to do the work, were best capable of leading others in the work. But, what is "the work" of Speculative Freemasonry? This is where it becomes necessary to pick a lane and decide on the path for a Lodge. If "the work" is the education of our candidates and members, then we take one path. If "the work" is only the enjoyment of the Lodge activities and possibly some charitable work, then we take another path. Both paths have successful Lodges.

The problem comes when we try to have the best of both worlds. If we desire to be a Lodge where real Masonic education takes place, but we operate as a social club, then we are doomed before we start. This situation brings constant frustration for all involved. In my experience, I've seen too many Lodges who simply cannot pick a lane and seem to want to be one thing, but not willing to do what is needed to be what they want.

I'll give a few observations that I have gleaned over the years. First, not everyone has to be a Lodge officer. The idea that one is not really worthy unless they have a "PM" behind their name is nonsense. We are not about gaining titles and honors. We are about learning and teaching. Second, not every good businessman is a good Lodge officer. Running a multi-million dollar business does not guarantee that you will be a good Lodge leader any more than being a good Lodge leader will qualify you to run a large, successful business. It's apples and oranges. To believe that business experience qualifies one for Lodge leadership is one of the main reasons, in my opinion, for Lodges going off in the wrong direction. So, what makes a good Lodge leader?

In my opinion, it goes back to the blueprint laid out in the *Old Charges*. It is the ones with the best abilities and merit. It is the ones who are best able to do the work. The work is in the broad sense the ritual, but we must be careful of the trap. If we view "the ritual" as the few lines of opening and closing the Lodge, then we are trapped. Knowing the ritual means not only the opening and closing, but all of the degree ritual as well as the meaning behind the ritual. The officers must be able to teach the meaning of the ritual to the young candidates. I mean *any* of the officers must be able to do this. They *all* must be able to stand in for any other officer and teach any of the ritual.

Many Lodges feel, and rightly know, that such an expectation is too much for their Lodge. Not everyone has the ability to learn the ritual, but all Lodges need officers every year. It is simply too much to expect all of their officers to know all of the ritual in a manner that they are not only considered proficient (or near it), but also have the ability to teach its meaning. They simply can't do it.

So, what happens? What do such Lodges do? Well, let's try to find that answer by looking at something else. What if you truly, deeply, and passionately want to be a concert pianist. You went every now and then to piano class, but had other interests. You never learned to play very well at all. But you still want to be a concert pianist. Guess what? That's not going to happen. So, you can be frustrated all of your life or you can join a music club, and at least try to enjoy some of the feeling of music. At some point, we have to get real.

Not every Lodge can be, wants to be, or needs to be, an educational, formal Masonic Lodge. A successful Lodge can be one where its members simply enjoy each other's company. Everyone need to be dead honest with themselves and properly evaluate themselves so that they can get the most out of every Masonic experience. We need to know ourselves, know who we are, what we are and always strive to be better tomorrow than we are today — by whatever standard we use.

Notes:

1. At least, in U.S. jurisdictions of which I am familiar.

Burning the Candle at Both Masonic Ends

I've always enjoyed studying the complexities of human nature. So often we see displays of remarkable accomplishments in places where we may rarely look for it. Over the last few years, I've also noticed something interesting occurring in Masonry. Originally, I thought it was a by-product of the effects from the declining membership. Maybe it is in part, but other factors seem to be playing into the equation. This situation is where you have a Mason who seems to be something of a double win. He's someone who is not only qualified and talented, but one with a sincere interest in helping out anywhere he can. He may be a new Mason or one who has been away for a number of years. It can really be any Mason who all of a sudden jumps in and *does* things. He does things *everywhere*. He is likely perceived by the lodge, and those around him, as someone who is valuable not only to their body but to the whole of Masonry.

So, let's look at this hard working Mason. His talent and willingness to become involved may be showcased in various leadership or ritualistic positions. But really, he can show up in any place or position where help is needed. You may start seeing this brother pop up in one lodge after another and then the York Rite, Scottish Rite – anywhere. When you walk in, there you will find him diligently at work. And then, maybe after a few years, something strange may happen. You can't find him anywhere. No one knows what happened to him. He is just gone. I think of this as Masonic burnout. I'd like to look at it a bit.

One of the first lessons we learn in Masonry is the lesson of the 24 inch gauge. This lesson is one of time management. It's about how we best use the day and divide up our time to most benefit from the hours within the day. And really, this lesson is part of a greater lesson of balance. If we can achieve balance in our life, we are able to do more and gain more from each day. After all, our goal as Masons is to always try and improve ourselves.

We must also understand that take there is a consequence for every action. A consequence can be positive or something far less desired. Even when our intentions are good and noble, the end result can be disappointing. Early in my Masonic career, I met a Mason who was respected not only for the work that he did but also as an educator. I was very fortunate to get to know him. He passed away a number of years ago, and I then became friends with his son. I remember talking with him about his dad. When you speak to someone about a family member, you gain the opportunity to learn things about them unknown to even friends. In this case, when I would ask questions about his father he would answer, but I could tell that there was always a little something that he held back in reserve. One day he opened up to me and said, "You have to try to understand my situation. Since I've become a Mason, I've come to realize a lot about my dad. I respect his accomplishments. He did a lot to help individual Masons and Masonry as a whole. But for me, he was my dad. I remember him growing up, and in all honesty, he was never there for me. He was never around. Every night of the week he was gone. It was either a lodge meeting, an appendant body, visiting with other Masons or something else. But he was always away doing something."

I thought about this situation for a good while. I began to realize that this respected brother, who had done so much for others, was seriously out of personal balance. All the good that he did for Masonry was tempered by the fact that he gave so little time to his family. The balance in life that we are taught to achieve was lost to this Brother. For all his good work, he did not personally benefit from our teachings.

So, are we really following the teachings of Freemasonry by spending all of our time helping others at the expense of not only ourselves but our family? We have to realize that there comes a time when we have to say no and not feel guilty about it. To try and be everywhere, all of the time, truly best serves no one.

The fact is that there is no way that any one individual can be everywhere that is needed. There are not enough hours in the day; there are not enough days in the week. The workers and leaders who are the most effective (to themselves and others) know how to choose where to go and how to properly manage their time. It is not a case of favoring one body over another; it is a matter of understanding personal limits and the consequences of going out of balance.

Masonic burnout comes into play when Masons take one job after another spreading themselves all over the Masonic landscape. Even if the physical stress or the stress on ones family life is minimal, there are other factors to consider. The odds are very slim that one who does ten jobs will be able to do all of them with the same level of quality as if he were only doing a few of them. We just do not do the same quality of work when we are spread so thin. In our sincere effort to help everyone, we may not be doing top quality work for anyone.

Now, what I have been discussing is a Mason who sincerely wishes to be of service to those in need. His problem is that he did not plan things out very well and ended up biting off more than he could possibly chew. In his desire to help, he failed to properly manage his time. The unexpected personal toll of being everywhere all the time often becomes too much for most anyone. But there is also a darker situation that should be discussed. This is the other type of Mason who you will also always find everywhere.

In the Scottish Rite craft degrees, the three "bad guys" are represented by three human failings: ignorance, falsehood, and ambition. Ambition, paired with ignorance and falsehood, is viewed as a lethal combination for morality. We must face the fact that some are driven to take part in Masonic work solely with the goal of personal gain. They seek power, titles, and glory. They will often work very hard to obtain what they seek. Like the sincere Mason who ends up burning himself out and disappears, so will the title seeking Mason often disappear when he obtains what he truly seeks. We should avoid these title and power seekers.

In the end, we must decide what we want out of Masonry and what we are willing to do to obtain our goal. Burning yourself out to show your love for Masonry will not make you a better Mason. It will also not truly help those who need your talent. It would seem far more effective if we spend our time in just a few places training others to do likewise. By helping and training others, the Masonic work can be performed in many more lodges who will have fresh Masons rendering any needed aid. One Mason doing everything can only go so far before he becomes burned out or the quality of the work suffers. Many Masons doing the work will result in a much longer ability to properly offer what is needed. Balance will be achieved and everyone wins.

Should We Allow EA's in Lodge Business Meetings?

Over the last few years a number of U.S. Grand Lodges have made a change in procedure for their Lodges. The change concerns how the Lodges conduct their business. But before we get into the change itself, I would like to talk just a bit about the concept of change itself. I find it very interesting how Grand Lodges go about making changes in their nature, policy, procedures, and laws.

Let's look at a pencil. It's really a handy and ingenious communication tool. On one end you have a sharp point. The inside writing material was originally made of lead, but today it's graphite. With this end you can write down whatever you want. It doesn't matter if you want to do a bit of calculus, an essay, or a love note — whatever you want to write, you can do so with the pencil. On the other end of the pencil is in an eraser. Use this end, and you can eliminate anything you have written in error simply by rubbing it a bit. Now, Grand Lodges operate pretty much the same way. They can make whatever decision they want. They can write whatever laws that they want and govern themselves however they see fit. But if at some point down the line they realize that something that they have done is not working best for them or not serving them as they expected, they can go back and erase it. They can go back to the way things were prior to changing the law, or they can go completely in another direction and do something different. That's the benefit of being a sovereign and independent Grand Lodge. They can write whatever laws they like, and if it doesn't work out as they desire, they can go back and change it. That is their prerogative.

Now, for longer than any Mason has been alive, Lodges in the United States have conducted their business in the Master Mason degree. But over the last ten or twelve years a number of jurisdictions in the United States decided that they wanted to change this practice. They wanted to give their Lodges the option of doing business in the Entered Apprentice, Fellowcraft, or Master Mason degree. Most of the jurisdictions that made this change felt that the degree in which the Lodge conducted its business should be left up to the Worshipful Master of the Lodge. Today, about half of the jurisdictions in the United States have made this change. The result is that there has been a good bit of discussion about this practice, its value, and if the rest of jurisdictions said should follow suit. Let's look a little at some of the history of how Lodges have conducted their business.

To start with, Lodges have not always conducted their business in the Master Mason degree. That was an innovation in the mid 1800's and something that is not done widely outside of the United States. The seeds of this innovation were planted around 1840. In 1843, there was a convention of Grand Lodge officers from the U.S. held in Baltimore, Maryland. This is normally known as the Baltimore Convention, but actually there were a number of such conventions that were held between 1843 and 1847. During this time, a lot of details were hammered out as to what would be the desired norm for Masonic jurisdictions in the United States. There was, also, a rekindling of the effort to have one Grand Lodge for the entire United States, but this was wisely voted down. A number of useful decisions did come out of this time, one being dues cards. It was felt that it would be beneficial for Masons to have dues cards to prove their current membership. Today, I doubt any U.S. jurisdiction would seriously consider giving up the practice of issuing dues cards. But some of the decisions turned out to be a bit of a hard sell. One initially unpopular decision was the concept that the business of a Lodge should be the concern only of Master Masons. It was felt that a Lodge of Master Masons should be the only degree in which the business of the Lodge should be discussed. Entered Apprentice and Fellowcraft Masons should no longer be present when business of the Lodge was discussed.

I find the decision to move from doing business on the Entered Apprentice degree to the Master Mason degree to be an interesting decision because of certain assumptions which were made which remain to this day in many areas. I'd like to look at some of these assumptions as well as how Lodges did operate prior to the 1840s.

Since I am most familiar with Louisiana Masonry, I'd like to look at the situation through the eyes of Louisiana Freemasonry. To start with, Louisiana was not part of the Baltimore convention. The Grand Lodge of Louisiana did not send representatives to any of the conventions. From what can be understood from the few early records that we have, it seems that Louisiana Masonry operated much like French Freemasonry. There were Lodges that worked in various languages as well as various Masonic rituals. This was just how we had always operated.

Lodges in Louisiana normally opened and conducted their business on the Entered Apprentice degree. When the FC or

MM degrees were going to be conferred, they had the option of opening in whatever degree they chose. Much was left to the discretion of the Worshipful Master. But, when we say that the Lodges conducted their business on the Entered Apprentice degree today, that creates misunderstandings today as to the role of the EA or FC Masons in these Lodges.

One of the key points that needs to be understood about early Louisiana Masonry is that so much of its early operation was based on the practices of French Freemasonry. This French practice would include a defined role for the Entered Apprentice and Fellowcraft Masons in the Lodge. In short, their job was to learn Freemasonry. Period. They were expected to learn all aspects of Freemasonry so that when they became a Master Mason, they would be fully qualified to participate with the other Masonic Masons in an intelligent manner. So, the Lodges in France, as well as Louisiana, would not only allow the Entered Apprentices and Fellowscrafts to come into the Lodge, but they would *expect* them to come in. They would sit in reserved areas and observe the operation of the Lodge. They did not speak or participate in any of the activities of the Lodge. They did not have the privilege of questioning anything, speaking in Lodge (unless they were answering a direct question from a MM), voting nor holding any office. They had one job to do in the Lodge — that was to observe and learn all that they could about the Lodge operation. They would quietly sit and watch the Master Masons conduct business.

Entered Apprentice and Fellowcraft Masons would often be assigned certain tasks or projects which would normally involve learning various aspects of the Masonic philosophy or symbolism. They would deliver lectures on what they learned with the Master Masons ready to challenge things in their lecture to be sure that they understood the work. While I have been addressing early French and Louisiana Masonry, this practice was certainly not limited to them alone. Most all of Freemasonry around the world operated much in this same manner. It was in this environment of learning and teaching that early Freemasonry existed.

Following the Baltimore Convention, Freemasonry in most areas of the United States became far more standard in practice. One area that became standard was the change in how business was conducted in the Lodge. Louisiana, not being part of the conventions, was a bit late with making this switch, and it was not until following 1850 did the Grand Lodge of Louisiana switch to conducting business on the Master Mason degree. After this time, I know of no U.S. jurisdiction that conducted business in any degree other than Master Mason. In earlier times, Freemasonry did not just initiate candidates into membership. Freemasonry taught its members in specific practices proven over time. Having Entered Apprentice Masons present during a business meeting was an excellent educational tool. So, what was the motivation to change to the Master Mason degree?

The desire for all of Masonry in the United States to be near copies of each other seems to have been matched by its desire to be unique in the world of Freemasonry. It seems we wanted to all be alike within the United States but different in many aspects from Masonry outside of the U.S. We did not want Lodges in any U.S. jurisdiction working in different rituals or different languages. We were also not afraid to make innovations from the norm of Masonic practice outside of the U.S. if we felt it was in our own best interest. It seems that the switch from doing business on the EA degree to the MM degree was one of these changes that simply wanted to be done.

I've heard interesting, but unproven theories as to why U.S. Masonry made the switch to conducting business on the MM degree. It was stated that because Freemasonry was hit so very hard during the so-called "Morgan Affair," the Lodges that survived, or were established after the events, wanted safeguards in place to lessen the chances of a repeat series of events. The feeling seems to have been that one who joined Masonry could not fully be trusted until he was a Master Mason. It seems the feeling could have been that the business of the Lodge was not for the ears or eyes of anyone but a Master Mason. It doesn't matter if this theory played a major part, contributing part, or no part at all, I find it an interesting theory. The fact is that the U.S. Masonic community did make the decision to switch from business on the EA to business on the MM degree. *Something* must have motivated them to do so.

Now, let's fast forward about 100 years to right after WWII. The war was over; there was peace for a time and things looked very promising for the United States. There was a swell in Masonic membership. The Grand Lodges accommodated the many new members by expanding the infrastructures of the various jurisdictions. I see this rapid growth as the birth of the "club mentality" in U.S. Freemasonry. But the increase in new members was not to last. By the 1970's, Grand Lodges saw a slowing and then diminishing of new members. They became worried about the large machines which had been created to handle all the new members. It was not a good time for U.S. Masonry.

Freemasonry in the U.S. struggled for a number of years until a string of bestselling books and movies came out starting in the 1980's & 90's with Freemasonry as the subject. They portrayed Freemasonry in a positive, if mysterious, light. All of a sudden, petitions started coming in to Lodges. Were the hard times over? Did we turn the corner and begin moving in the right direction? Maybe, but maybe not.

While the number of petitions took a dramatic upswing, the number of demits and suspensions for non-payment of dues over the next years was also noteworthy. It would seem that while many joined, they soon left. Why?

It would seem that the books and movies portrayed Freemasonry as a group of enlightened mystics with something akin to the secrets of life as the reward for joining. And what was found in too many Lodges? A group of old men reading minutes and arguing over bills. There was absolutely nothing mystical or esoteric in the meetings. No enlightenment, no education, no inspiring members teaching life lessons — nothing but donuts and coffee. Not only were the meetings far from enlightening, they were far from interesting. It was not a matter of the Lodge experience failing to be *everything* that they expected; it was nothing of what they expected. So, they left.

But, not everyone left. A small group of young Masons did remain. They clearly see the lacking in the Lodges. They work towards (and hope upon hope to see) a change in operation. The problem is that the lack of anything significant has become the accepted Lodge experience. Too many older Members do not want education, or symbolic study, or anything but the way things are in the Lodge. Short of a revolution, or waiting for funerals, what can the young ones do?

Because many Lodges are suffering from lack of qualified members going through the chairs, new Masons joining are snapped up for Lodge office if they show the slightest bit of potential. Even before they know the difference between Speculative Freemasonry and Operative Freemasonry, they are the Worshipful Master. It is here that the new members can benefit from the old way of doing things in Masonry.

If the young, new Masons have the opportunity of just observing the operation of the Lodge they will have the six or eight months (average) time between their EA initiation and their MM degree to gather some idea of Lodge operation. They will be far more experienced than a brand new MM with no idea as to Lodge operation being thrown into office right after their degree. It's very true that if nothing else changes, many of these might drop out before receiving their Master Mason degree. Of course, the lacking in too many Lodges will also be realized and some will find it unworthy of their time – but not all. The ones who remain will be more experienced.

Look, unless you have your head buried in the sand, we all know that there is something seriously wrong in too many Lodges. It's not too late to turn things around, but we need to act – now. We are an Order that provides moral education to its members by symbolic instruction following initiations. We are special. We are not a club to feed the egos of old men who just want to be somebody or want to gather with friends a couple of times a month for social visits. We have a responsibility to who and what we claim to be. We can either do what is right, or be a part of the problem.

Business meetings with EA's and FC's should never be with the goal of giving a voice or vote to those who are not MM's. A vote and vote in the Lodge as well as its leadership is for experienced Master Masons. The role of EA's and FC's is to sit quietly and learn. Period. It is the duty of MM's to teach the less informed. Every meeting of the Lodge is an opportunity for education. Just like physical exercise, the more we do it, the better our Masonic health. Step by step we can improve.

What each Grand Lodge does, is ultimately up to them. We can take whatever direction we wish to take, or, we can flounder with inaction. The choice is always ours. My hope is that we choose education and do all we can, by every means possible, to make sure we educate our members and give them every chance to be what we should be — educated Freemasons.

When Masons Come Knocking - Visiting Masons

This paper will discuss visitors in Lodges. But for our purposes, visiting a Lodge means a Lodge at Labor. A Lodge function such as Bring a Friend Night, Ladies Night, Awards Night, or any type of public event will be done either before or after the Lodge is opened or closed or during refreshment.

Bringing non-Masons into a Lodge at Labor is never allowed and can result in Masonic discipline by your Grand Lodge. There is a procedure for trying anyone seeking to visit your Lodge that is prescribed by your Grand Lodge. Follow the rules and regulations of your Grand Lodge for testing anyone who wishes to visit your Lodge during a business meeting or degree.

Fraternal Relations are also an issue and Lodges should have a printed book, material, or on-line access to where they can verify if the Lodge of a visitor is recognized by your Grand Lodge. For the balance of this paper, it will be assumed that all tests and trials have been successfully completed for any visitor to your Lodge.

For questions on how to properly examine someone seeking to attend your Lodge, how to determine if a Lodge is recognized by your Grand Lodge, or any of the questions as to if a visitor is qualified to visit your Lodge at labor, please contact your Grand Secretary's office where the proper information for your Grand Lodge will be provided. I strongly advise you not to assume anything in regard to visitors and to follow all rules, customs, and laws of your Grand Lodge. If you are not sure of anything, find out from your Grand Lodge.

Since Masons call each other Brothers, there is a suggestion of family. It is not so much of a stretch to equate a Lodge with our home. In each of our homes we have certain customs that may be particular to our own family. Likewise, Lodges may have their own customs as well. One thing, however, is common in all homes or Lodges – we extend politeness and respect to visitors and expect the same from them.

A visitor to your home, or your Lodge, is expected to respect your customs and practices. Likewise, you want all visitors to feel welcome and you want them to know that you appreciate their taking the time to visit you. While the members of the Lodge can contribute to making a visitor feel welcome, the two officers who have the most responsibility once the Lodge goes to labor are the Worshipful Master and the Senior Deacon.

Now, I realize that some Lodges are in trouble and the office of Senior Deacon might well be occupied by someone either brand new to Masonry or by someone who just happened to be there on election night and agreed to accept the position. This may result in the Senior Deacon of some Lodges having little to no experience in, or knowledge of, the office. Since, with the exception of degrees, the Senior Deacon does not have a speaking part for most all of the duties during the opening or closing of a Lodge, there is sometimes a misguided feeling that *anyone* can hold this position. Sometimes very little is expected from someone offered the position. During degrees, the Senior Deacon is often replaced by someone who does know the work.

But the problems come when the inexperienced Senior Deacon is called upon to receive visitors. It is usually an embarrassing situation to watch a Senior Deacon who has no clue how to properly receive visitors stumble through a basic introduction.

Truthfully, there is no excuse for Senior Deacons not knowing how to receive visitors. The blame for a Senior Deacon woefully ignorant of his duties lies not only with him for not learning the work, but also with the Worshipful Master who has not made sure that he knows the work or replaced him with someone who does.

Regular Lodges of instruction where particular emphasis is placed on how to properly introduce and receive visitors to the Lodge should be held. A Junior Deacon who does not know how to fill in for the Senior Deacon and perform all of his duties should not be advanced to the office of Senior Deacon when the time comes. Excuses that the Lodge has no one available to fill these positions and has to take anyone available, with or without knowledge or experience of the position, only exposes the Lodge as one that has failed in its basic duties.

A successful Lodge will insist that appointed offices know their duties and perform them with a high degree of proficiency. A successful Lodge will also insist that elected offices also know their duties and perform them with a high degree of proficiency or they will not be elected to the next office come election night.

The concept that loyalty demands that you keep someone in office and advance them simply because they accepted a position and show up, with no concern over their ability, or lack of it, is a misguided sense of loyalty that quickly drives nails into the coffin of any Lodge. Such unfortunate beliefs can contribute significantly to a Lodge's eventual failure. Our loyalty should be to our Lodge and whatever is in the best interest of the Lodge.

The Worshipful Master sets the tone for how visitors should be received and many times Lodge customs come into play. For example, in some Lodges, visitors are asked to stand and introduce themselves. Once this is done, the Worshipful Master will say a few words welcoming the visitor and then move on to other business. In other Lodges, the custom may be to call upon the Senior Deacon to escort a visitor west of the altar and have the introduction and welcoming words done there.

If the Visitor is a dignitary or holds any office in the Grand Lodge, the Worshipful Master may invite him to a seat in the East. This is at the pleasure of the Worshipful Master, and truthfully, unless your Grand Lodge has particular rules guiding a Worshipful Master, then anyone could be invited for a seat in the East.

The Worshipful Master, as well as the Senior Deacon, should be proficient as to giving Grand Honors and the ceremony involved with it. The way to become proficient is to practice. Most jurisdictions will have this ceremony explained in their monitors and there will be a public and private ceremony available depending on if the Lodge is at labor or if the Grand Honors are to be given during a public event. The Lodge should practice these ceremonies so that all involved will have a high degree of proficiency. Fewer things are more embarrassing for a Lodge then when a Grand Master or one from his official family visits a Lodge and the Lodge stumbles through what should be a smooth ceremony.

A successful Worshipful Master will make time during a slow business night to rehearse this simple, but important, ceremony with all members involved.

One thing that should be recognized by everyone, and by this I mean Lodges receiving visitors as well as visitors themselves, is that jurisdictions each have their own customs and titles that are given to past and present officers. For example, I am a Past Master and a Past District Grand Lecturer of the Grand Lodge of Louisiana. When addressed in Lodge, I am usually addressed as "Worshipful Brother." This is the same way a current District Grand Lecturer would be addressed, but not everywhere.

I lived for about ten years in Virginia. I remember the first Lodge I visited there. Before the meeting, I was questioned as to any Lodge or Grand Lodge offices that I held. I told them the offices I had held. After the Lodge was opened, the Worshipful Master instructed the Senior Deacon to conduct me west of the altar. I was introduced as Right Worshipful Brother Michael Poll, given the private Grand Honors and escorted to the East. I was rather surprised, but said nothing until the Lodge was over.

After the Lodge closed, I thanked the Worshipful Master for his kindness, but mentioned that I am not addressed as "Right Worshipful Brother" in Louisiana. The District Deputy Grand Master happened to be present and overheard me talking to the Master. He jumped in and said "Well, you are not in Louisiana right now, are you?" He then explained to me that in Virginia, anyone who has served in any office *at all* in the Grand Lodge is addressed as "Right Worshipful Brother." This would include any current or Past Grand Lodge officer and the title would remain for life. I felt a bit awkward, but this was their custom.

The other side of the coin, however, would be one who is a past Grand Lodge officer in a jurisdiction that uses such titles and then visits a Lodge under a jurisdiction that does not offer such titles to past Grand Lodge appointive officers. I have seen one case where a Brother appeared insulted when he was addressed as "Worshipful Brother" rather than "Right Worshipful Brother" as he was accustomed. I really believe that this falls into the category of "get over yourself." If we place such importance in titles that we become insulted if we do not receive every single title that we believe we are do, then I believe we have missed some of the very basic teachings in Masonry. On the other hand, does it really cost us anything to address someone by a title that is not customary in our jurisdiction but is customary in theirs?

I believe it all comes down to basic politeness. Visitors should be polite and appreciative of any consideration given to them by a Lodge they visit. They should expect and demand nothing and should conduct themselves with respect towards the Lodge. The same should be extended by the Lodge to all visitors. Politeness and respect is a two-way street.

A successful Lodge is one that will receive and accommodate visitors with all due respect and welcome them as Brothers. The Worshipful Master should make the reception of all visitors a priority and extend to them every courtesy from the Lodge. Make them feel welcome and special. Let them know that the time they took to visit you is appreciated. Have their name, Lodge, and any offices they hold recorded by the secretary. Giving them a small gift or token of the Lodge is always a nice touch. I have several gifts given to me by Lodges that I treasure.

If you visit a Lodge, make sure you dress properly and show all respect to the Lodge and its officers. If we just take a little time to show that we appreciate visiting or being visited, the whole experience becomes infectious and fraternal bonds are formed and grow. We all win.

Who are you? Who am I?

Since boyhood, I have been given two pieces of advice. I was always told to try to make a good first impression and that I should trust my first impression of others. After considerable thought, I'm not so sure that I agree with these bits of guidance in today's world. It's not that I disagree that first impressions dictate how many form their opinion of others. I'm just not so sure that this advice is something beneficial for me. It's the variables that I find to be a problem. How do I know if "you" are "you" or a created persona? Let me explain. Some years ago, I "met" someone on-line and read a number of things that he posted on various forums. Frankly, I was turned off. That was my first impression. He seemed to be always angry and nasty to others. He acted like a schoolyard bully. After reading many of his on-line posts, I had the opportunity to meet him in person. He was nothing at all like his posts. He was a very nice, amiable man. How can this be explained? Were the on-line posts the "real" him? Was the "real" person the one I met and the on-line rants just an on-line character he created? Maybe he is a combination of the two personalities? I just can't say without getting to know him better. And maybe that is the whole point. Maybe we do ourselves (and others) a disservice by "first impression" evaluations.

We live in a world today where everything seems to be fast. No more do we put a pen to paper, write a letter to a friend, and mail it at the post office. We would normally wait a few weeks before we wondered why they had not answered us. Today we may send an email or text in the morning and wonder why they have not answered us by the afternoon. Our cars, trains, and planes go faster, and even our food is heated much faster in our microwaves. I have to wonder if society as a whole always benefits from the new world of instant gratification.

I won't suggest that it is impossible to correctly size someone up in a very short time, nor will I say that love at first sight does not exist. I am only saying that for me, I much prefer my coffee in a nice cup, sitting down, and slowing savoring every drop of it. Aside from a caffeine rush, gulping down my coffee from a paper cup while I rush through traffic in my car is no pleasurable or memorable event. But these are just my feelings.

I'm not opposed to everything being done quickly, but I do find value in slowing down and taking our time with certain things. I believe that something as important as understanding others deserves more than a quick look and snap judgement. I do find value in sitting down and enjoying that slow, good cup of coffee with someone while I try to get to know them better. I trust in this method far more than forming my opinions based on writings by them on this or that forum. But we *are* in a world of "let's get it done quickly." Others may not be so slow with the forming of their opinions. This is why I believe it is so important to be careful with things that we write or share online. Regardless of who we truly are, the image we project online is accepted by far too many as the *real* us. And opinions are often formed very quickly and become truth for many.

There is a good reason why most all Grand Lodges have rules governing on-line communications. As Freemasons, how we conduct ourselves on-line reflects on the whole of Freemasonry. Angry, profanity laced, displays bordering on frenzied rage does not exactly fit with one who claims to be a "Seeker of Light." In fact, some Grand Lodges have determined that over the top on-line displays should result in Masonic discipline. This is especially true when the one writing with such anger posts under the name of, or tied to, the on-line page of a Masonic lodge.

To be a balanced Mason requires one to understand how we are seen as well as how we see others. I often heat up my frozen lunch quickly in a microwave. But I also try to take my time when I seek to understand the nature of another. I believe that it is the balance of knowing when to act quickly and when to take our time that brings us the most reward.

When the Best Help is to Walk Away

One of the biggest frustrations that individual Masons have with Lodges has to do with the direction that the Lodges are going. The question of right and wrong, as far as to the direction of the Lodge, is very subjective. What's right for one Lodge may be completely wrong for the other. The correct direction for a Lodge is the direction desired by most of the members. It is not necessary that all Lodges do as you like, in fact it's not possible. Because individuals have different likes and dislikes, you're going to find different paths taken by different Lodges. Of course there is a new wave of Masonry taking place. The deeper aspects of Masonic philosophy, history, and ritual are desired to be taught in the Lodges by more members than in the recent past. But there are also many Lodges which are more or less social or charity clubs. The members gather together for an evening of conversation, maybe over a meal, and then some talk to plan a worthy charitable or social project. There is nothing in the world wrong with this type of Lodge, unless the members want something more. There is also nothing in the world wrong with the Lodge that teaches Masonic philosophy. This would be a Lodge where at any meeting you may find some lecture on any one of the deeper aspects of Freemasonry. The problems come when you are in one type of Lodge and expect something else from your Lodge experience. Each of these problems would not necessarily be a problem of the Lodge, but a problem for you as an individual. If you are not satisfied, or happy, with what goes on in your Lodge, yet the Lodge is functioning well, has good attendance and all the signs of success then how can anyone say that the Lodge is doing something wrong? There is a big difference between a Lodge that is floundering, has no direction, and cannot see a successful future for itself, and the Lodge that simply operates differently than some may desire.

If you are not satisfied with the direction your Lodge is going, but it is clear that the Lodge is operating successfully, then the problem is yours. Trying to change such a Lodge to suit your desires is not only unfair but rarely possible. Even if you were able to change such a Lodge to make you personally happy, it would likely result in the majority of the members becoming unhappy and the future success of the Lodge could be at question.

We need to realistically look at a situation without emotion, and try to determine the best course of action for us as individuals. There is no shame in realizing that a successful Lodge is going in a direction not desired by you. There is no shame in finding a new Lodge. Charges that you are being unfair, disloyal, or ungrateful to your Lodge because you leave are unfounded, spoken without knowledge, and should be disregarded. Everyone has the right to have their own desired Masonic experience. If, however, it is clear that your Lodge is in trouble then you should do all that you can to try and help your Lodge. When someone puts out their hand and asks for your help, whenever possible you should try to help them. But, you should note what I just said, as well as noting the qualifying phrase and obligations. The qualifying phrase is, "whenever possible." Let me try to explain.

I remember long ago as a boy hearing loud, angry yelling outside my house. I went outside and saw a neighbor doing something very strange. He was staggering down the middle of the street with his head back and arms outstretched yelling like a wild man. As a child that sight shook me. My mother came out, grabbed me, and pulled me back into the house. She told me to stay inside and locked the door. She told me that the neighbor was "ill." Years later she told me more about that story. The neighbor was an alcoholic. His wife had done everything that could be done to try and help him. He would listen to no one. Finally, after going to therapy, fighting with him, threatening him, and doing everything possible, the therapist had a stern conversation with the wife. He told her that there was nothing more that she could do to reach her husband. He said that unless *he* decided to change, he was not going to change. He said that unless he made the decision to stop, he was going to continue to drink himself to death. He said that there was nothing that she could do to force him to change or stop. He told the wife that there was only one thing that she could do if she cared about him. She agreed to do it. She took all of the money out of the checking account, went to the grocery, and stocked the refrigerator, freezer, and cabinets with food. She made sure there was not a drop of liquor in the house, and she left him. The therapist said it was necessary for him to reach rock bottom in order to help him. What I saw coming down the street as a boy was the husband reaching rock-bottom. The wife could no longer reason with him. She was blamed by him for all of his troubles by leaving him. He had broken into the house of another neighbor, stolen all of his liquor, and was yelling at his wife, and the world, in the middle of the street.

What has this to do with a Lodge that's in trouble? Well, we all have free will. Many times we see, believe, and think whatever we want. If the Lodge is in trouble, and by that I mean, low attendance, trouble filling chairs, in need of calling other Lodges for degree work, and all the problems that go along with disinterest in a Lodge, then the Lodge may or may not recognize that they are in serious trouble.

If the Lodge does not recognize that they are in trouble, or refuses to do what is needed to bring them back to health, then anyone who tries to help them may be seen as the troublemaker. They may be seen as the problem. Whatever they say or suggest should be done will be seen *as* the problem. The Lodge would be in denial of their real problem and what is needed to fix it. They cannot be reached and if someone pushes them to make this or that change in order to help them, not only will the Lodge not do as advised, but they will get angry or see the one giving advice as the problem. In such a case, to continue to try and help will only cause more problems. You need to back away from them and allow them to see the problem for themselves or fail as a Lodge.

We must do all we can to help anyone who asks for help. We must also respect that everyone has the right to do as they desire. We should never try to force our will on another.

If we are in a situation that we know is not right for us and the Lodge does not wish to change, then we should find a new Lodge. If the Lodge does not wish to change because they are successful in what they are doing, wish them well and move on. If they are in obvious trouble and you realize that if they do not change, they will possibly fail at some point, then take a few extra steps with them. Try to make them see that it is in their best interest to change. However, we must realize that there is a point when offering help becomes harassment. No matter how much we may want to help, we must realize that sometimes the very best help we can give is to walk away. No matter how much it hurts we cannot help someone who does not want to be helped. By pushing help, we may not only aggravate a bad situation, but we may be denying others who are ready and willing to accept our help. We have to know when a desire to help becomes a desire to get our own way. Walking away is sometimes the most Masonic thing that can be done.

Be the Scottish Rite

As with Lodges, some Scottish Rite valleys have low attendance, lack of interest by the members, and generally a lack of support for pretty much anything that the valley does.

In the Southern Jurisdiction, members who distinguish themselves by work are often recognized by being given what's known as a cap. You may see 32nd degree Masons in a valley wearing a black pillbox cap that has been given to them by the valley reflective of work they have done. Or you may see a distinctive black cap worn by someone who is a member of the Knights of St. Andrew. A 32nd degree Mason who has received the distinction of Knight Commander of the Court of Honour will wear a red cap. One who has received the 33rd degree and is an Honorary Sovereign Grand Inspector General, will wear a white cap.

Some years back, an elderly Mason pointed out to me that if you want to see a valley that's in trouble look around at the members present at any valley meeting. If more than half of those present are wearing caps, of any color, then the valley is in trouble. It means that the ones who are showing up have been given something. A successful valley will bring in members who have received no distinction at all but are there simply because they enjoy what's going on.

So, what problems can a valley face?

Basically, they face the same problems that a Lodge would face. This would come from disinterest by the members in what's going on, and/or a lack of good leadership.

I've visited a number of valley meetings over the years in a number of states and the ones that seem to be in trouble do seem to be almost identical to each other. The members present at a meeting will likely see someone other than the presiding officer pretty much running the meeting, giving instructions to everyone, and setting the tone for the meeting.

The meeting will consist of a bare-bones agenda with little more than a reading of the minutes, discussion of who was sick, or who has died, and ideas of what can be done to improve attendance or build up membership.

In some valleys we find considerable work on what can, basically, be called gimmicks designed to create interest in the valley. These gimmicks span a wide range of events, some done at meetings and others more along the lines of field trips. I've seen field trips such as picnics, trips to museums, movies, dinners out, cruises, gathering members who enjoy golf and even baseball. Pretty much anything that you can do outside seems to have been tried by some valley trying to build interest in their valley.

I was told of one valley that was having low attendance and lacking interest in the valley meetings. When the valley was told that they should have presentations made during the meetings, a slideshow was shown one night of photos someone had taken on their vacation. There was actually surprise when it didn't draw that much interest.

Other ideas of limited success were ladies nights, dances, game nights, and even one valley tried karaoke night. When all of these efforts failed, the membership was sometimes blamed for not supporting the valley. The leadership in these valleys *just doesn't get it.*

Let me try to explain this with an analogy.

Let's say that a new sporting goods store opens up in your neighborhood. It looks to be like a place that has a lot of potential. So when the place opens up, you go and pay them a visit. Maybe you need some new fishing gear, golf clubs, or something else.

When you get to the store and start walking down the aisles, you're met with a surprise. All you see on any of the shelves are boxes of cookies. In fact, every type of cookie you can imagine is on the shelves. There's nothing wrong with the cookies and they do have a large selection of cookies, but this is a sporting goods store. You came here to buy sporting goods, not cookies. Do you see?

Scottish Rite Masons come to a valley meeting to experience the *Scottish Rite*, not to sing karaoke or just listen to minutes of who died or complaints about why no one is attending. They come to the *Scottish Rite* for a *Scottish Rite* experience. Just like in a Lodge, your choice is either give them what they want or to watch them walk away. It's as simple as that. If you don't know how to give them *a real* Scottish Rite experience, then, excuse me but what in the world are you doing holding office?

We cannot blame *the members* if they have better things to do than attend our boring meetings. Well, truthfully *we can* and sometimes *do* blame them, but it's not going to do us any good. We can either give them what they want (and what they paid for) or we can watch as they walk away.

If you are in a leadership position in your Valley, then you probably have seen this book. It's the *Scottish Rite Ritual Monitor and Guide* by Arturo de Hoyos.[1] I suggest that you read it, study it, and make use of it in your valley. If you want a program for your valley, create one from this book. If for some unimaginable reason, you don't have a copy of it, I've provided a link where you can order it at the end of this paper. This is the book that will teach you what you need to know about the Scottish Rite, and by using it can help you create interest in your valley.

The Scottish Rite has an unbelievable collection of degrees filed with the type of symbolism highly desired by the young Masons. In the world of sales, the Scottish Rite should be a very easy sell. The Scottish Rite is *exactly* what is desired by so many of the young Masons.

Their frustration comes when their Scottish Rite experience turns out to be old men acting important who know *nothing* of the Scottish Rite philosophy and are clearly only trying to impress everyone with how much of a big shot they are. Young men come to the Scottish Rite *to learn* the Scottish Rite and *experience* the Scottish Rite. It's really not rocket science.

If you want a successful Scottish Rite valley, then ***give them*** the Scottish Rite. If you don't know the Scottish Rite, *learn the Scottish Rite* or step aside. Don't give the membership nonsense and then blame them for not coming to the meetings.

I happen to deeply care about the Scottish Rite. It is a source of personal frustration when I receive emails or see situations that should be easy to understand and fix, but are made impossibly complex simply because people who don't *want* to do anything but what *they* want to do – blame everyone else for their problems.

No Masonic body, and that includes a Scottish Rite valley, either succeeds or fails because of one person. It's always a group effort. To have a successful Scottish Rite valley *be a* Scottish Rite valley. If you don't know what that means, learn more about the Scottish Rite.

The choice is yours.

Notes:

1. de Hoyos, Arturo. *Scottish Rite Ritual Monitor and Guide*. Washington, DC: The Supreme Council, 33°, 2010.

http://www.scottishritestore.org

The Lodge Meal

Over the years, I've written a good bit about the importance of Masonic education in Lodges. I've talked about how some Lodges offer little more than a hot meal and a reading of the minutes. For those Masons desiring more out of their Masonic experience, this sort of Lodge is a tremendous disappointment. But I don't want to be misunderstood. So that my meaning is perfectly clear, I believe Masons deserve much more than a meal and minutes, but in no way do I mean that a good meal at Lodge is unimportant. I believe that a good meal should be *part* of a total experience which should include Masonic education.

Human Beings are social creatures, and we enjoy the company of each other. In today's world, we don't really *need* Masonic Lodges to study Masonic books, but the exchange of ideas with our fellow Masons *is* of benefit to us. Being with other Masons is not only for our education, but also for the enjoyment of learning with others. As Masons, and as humans, we benefit from being with others of like mind and sharing thoughts and ideas. A good meal to start off the Lodge experience is nothing but beneficial for everyone.

For the balance of this paper, I am going to assume that following the meal, the Members will go up to their Lodge and benefit further from a sound educational program in the Lodge.

So, let's focus on the meal.

Now, in my traveling around, I've seen many different types of Lodges. I've seen massive multi-story temples in large cities and small cinder-block buildings with just a couple of rooms out in the middle of nowhere. Some Lodges have large, fully stocked kitchens and even barbeque areas outside. Other Lodges are so small that they are lucky if they have a coffee pot. But everyone eats, and there are ways to work a great dinner experience no matter the limitations of your Lodge.

As with everything else, planning is key. If you fly by the seat of your pants and just expect things to work out, then they probably won't. A smart Junior Warden will start planning out his year as WM even though he is several years away from the office.

As far as meals go, think about variety and quality. If you don't plan things out and have a schedule for meals, then real life will get in the way and on meeting night, you will be rushing to the grocery to buy hot dogs to throw in a large pot of water — *great, memorable meal.*

I suggest that a meal committee be formed and it be an active committee. Lodges normally meet once or twice a month. It is not that hard to plan out meals a good bit ahead of time and stick to a schedule. Many times where you live and where the Lodge is located will play a part in the types of meals you serve.

Lodges near large bodies of water will normally have seafood readily available. Large pots of stew or really large pots of whatever is a local favorite is good. You want to have enough food to feed everyone and then a bit extra — just in case.

I remember one Lodge that decided that they were going to place more emphasis on good meals. They were tired of hot dogs, cold cuts, and spaghetti and meat balls. They wanted more variety in their meals. By luck, an amateur chef joined their Lodge and offered to cook for them. In just a few months, the Lodge was the talk of the area and attendance did go up quite a bit. In fact, the whole atmosphere of the Lodge turned from *ho-hum* to excited to be there.

I realize that not every Lodge has an amateur or professional chef as a member, but there are other things you can do. Get yourself a good cookbook and use it. A few years ago, I edited *Lodge Cooking*[1] a cookbook designed for Masonic Lodges. But really any good cookbook will work. The key is to make sure that you like the type of food in a cookbook and that the recipes lend themselves to expansion. By this I mean, if the recipe says that it's for three people, make sure that the ingredients lend themselves to doubling, tripling, or whatever is needed to equal the number of people you expect at a meeting. Simple ingredient measurements are far easier to multiply than complicated ones.

The idea is to create excitement in the type of meals that will be served so that the meals themselves will be an event and not just something that you do before Lodge. A boring meal before Lodge sets a bad tone for the rest of the evening, whereas an enjoyable meal can turn everything around.

Advertising good, upcoming meals in your Lodge newsletter also builds interest. I remember one Scottish Rite valley where the secretary made it an event when reading the minutes to talk about the previous meal. He talked of the "succulent and tender roast beef" with a "fresh and exciting side salad" and other phrases that would make anyone who had missed the last meeting envious of what they missed.

It all comes down to working as a team to make all aspects of the Lodge experience enjoyable and something you don't want to miss. But there is one thing more that I really need to mention.

Let's go back for a moment and talk about the Lodge I commented on that had the amateur chef who volunteered to cook for them. Yes, without question, he cooked some outstanding meals for the Lodge. Everyone enjoyed the cooking and attendance did go up considerably because of the dramatic improvement in the quality of the meals. Members did begin looking forward to the meal, and it did become a major part of the whole Lodge experience.

But after about a year the young brother stopped showing up at Lodge, and no longer offered to cooked for them. The members of the Lodge were upset and some actually said that he was letting the Lodge down by refusing to cook for them.

So, why did he stop cooking?

The reason is not so hard to understand. He went to considerable effort on his own to plan out the meals, go to the grocery, buy everything, show up at Lodge at least an hour or two early to cook the meal, serve the meal to the members and then, by himself, remain after the Lodge was over to clean all the pots and pans that were used to cook the meal.

He was not paid to cook for the Lodge and was only reimbursed for the food that he purchased. The members would show up at Lodge, eat the food, enjoy themselves and then go to the Lodge. They would never help him pick up the food from the grocery, help him with any of the cooking, nor any of the cleaning up after Lodge and most of the time did not even thank him for what he did. He felt taken advantage of and grew tired of what seemed to be the wholly unappreciated work that he was doing.

It shouldn't have to be said, but if someone is going out of their way to help you, let them know how much you appreciate their efforts. Don't leave them on their own and not even acknowledge what they are doing for you.

A successful lodge is one that not only provides programs, events and education for its members, but lets all who help them know how much they are valued and how much they appreciate their efforts. Not showing appreciation for what someone does is a very quick way for them to realize that they could be spending their time in much better ways.

If you are going to do something, you might as well do it right. By spending a little time to plan out your Lodge meals and treating it as an event itself, you can make so much more out of it. Planning is key. Be creative. Look around at what successful Lodges are doing. Try new things. Create budgets for meals just as you would for any necessary expense.

If you charge for meals, make sure it just covers the expense and also make sure that what they are getting is something they are happy to pay for. I know of one Lodge that made a deal with a meat processing plant and obtained some very nice steaks at a great price. They served barbeque steaks with baked potatoes and charged $5.00 a head. They covered all their expenses, including drinks and everyone had a great time.

I saw another Lodge that charged the same price for boiled hot dogs and chips. Guess which Lodge was the happier?

Notes:

1. Poll, Michael R., Ed. *Lodge Cooking*. New Orleans, LA: Cornerstone Book Publishers, 2016.

Masonic Jurisprudence – the Laws of Freemasonry

I believe the best way to look at Masonic law, or if you wish, its philosophy, Masonic jurisprudence, is to view it as the things that are proper to do or improper to do in Masonry. This could mean the operation of a Lodge or the conduct of individual Masons inside or out of the Lodge.

Masonic law could deal with our relationship with the Grand Lodge, any of its officers; our own Lodge, any of its officers; as well as individual Masons. Masonic law also plays a part in how we interact with non-Masons and how we conduct ourselves in general society.

I believe that it is indispensable for all Masons to have read and be familiar with their Lodge bylaws as well as the Grand Lodge handbook of Masonic law – or whatever name is given to the publication of the rules and regulations of your Grand Lodge. With this basic information, we can navigate the proper operation of the Lodge and conduct ourselves in a manner in accordance with Freemasonry as practiced in most jurisdictions.

There are a few aspects of Lodge operation that I would like to particularly cover in this paper. I would also like, at the beginning, to mention that because each jurisdiction is sovereign and independent, Masonic law varies from jurisdiction to jurisdiction. While there are a good number of generally accepted procedures that will be used by many to most jurisdictions, it is dangerous to represent *anything* as the law of all Masonry. The final authority on any rule, regulation or law of Masonry is your own Grand Lodge. The only thing that I will say in this paper that definitely applies to everyone, is that you should read, learn, and follow the rules and regulations of your Grand Lodge.

The first aspect of Lodge operation and law that I would like to talk about is a procedure that we have all gone through prior to joining Masonry. This would be the process from the investigation committee to the ballot box.

I believe that the actions of an investigation committee as well as those who ballot on a candidate, may well be the most profound and sobering actions that we take in Masonry. When we stop and think about this, we are passing judgment on the worthiness of another human being. How in the world can we be qualified to do such a thing? And yet it is something we must do.

Any thinking person will realize what a tremendous and awesome responsibility is placed upon us. I can think of no way to disrespect Masonry greater than an investigation committee that is lax or negligent in their duties.

The sad truth of the matter is that I have seen far too many investigation committees who do little more than learn the name of the candidate and his address. The investigation of a candidate, if we can call it that, is far more often than not, left to a third-party paid investigation service. These investigation companies provide the basic information about a candidate and then inform the Lodge if the candidate shows up in their records as being arrested for any crime. Time after time, in many areas, such paid investigation companies are shown to provide incorrect or incomplete information. Lodges pay for these services and accept the information received as fact, no matter if it is or not. And yet, far too many lodges use such companies as their *sole* manner of investigating a candidate.

Grand Lodges apparently know that if they did not require this basic investigation, then there is a good chance that *no* investigation *at all* would take place in too many Lodges. How sad.

An investigation committee should be composed of at least three members of the Lodge, one of them being a knowledgeable Past Master. They should understand the significance and responsibility they have to both the Lodge and the whole of Freemasonry.

If paid investigation services are used, then they should be the start, not the end, of the investigation. The investigation committee should have no preconceived opinion of the candidate. They should simply investigate him with an open mind to see if he is worthy to be considered a member of their own family — a brother.

The members of an investigation committee must know the laws of Masonry. They should be dedicated, sincere, have no biases, and be totally committed to fairly investigating the candidate in a manner respectful to both the Lodge and the candidate.

If the Lodge does not have qualified members capable of serving conscientiously on an investigation committee, then frankly, why does the Lodge exist? The choices are to do the job correctly, learn *how* to do it correctly, or close shop. This responsibility is too great to be entrusted to those with limited Masonic knowledge or to those with less than noble intentions.

And now we come to the ballot box. I believe there is no greater test of the integrity of a Mason and no greater trust *in* that integrity than with the ballot box. I don't believe any instruction on how to use the ballot box is necessary here as it certainly has been explained to all Masons in their Lodge. But I will point out that *because* the balloting is done in secret, at least in all jurisdictions of which I am familiar, a special trust is displayed. The Lodge places full trust in the integrity of all Masons that they will ballot in the best interest of Freemasonry and with the honor expected of Freemasons.

Because the ballot is secret, that trust is backed up by the inability to expose anyone who may violate the integrity of the ballot box. Anyone who would use the ballot box in an unMasonic manner is protected by the secrecy of the ballot. They will only answer in the next world for their actions.

Because lodges of Freemasons have Masonic trial, it is obvious that not all who join completely understand, or wish to follow, the teachings of Freemasonry. Simply put, we *do* have bad apples among us. There are times when jealousy, revenge, bigotry, or any one of many less than noble reasons influence someone to misuse the ballot box to the detriment of all.

If someone knows of a valid reason why someone should not be allowed to join us, then this information should be shared with the Master of the Lodge where the candidate has petitioned or the investigation committee.

We have a responsibility to Freemasonry to see that none join us who are morally unfit or for any other valid reason would be viewed as unsuitable for Freemasonry. This is a responsibility that we owe to Freemasonry, the Lodge, and all Masons who have gone before us. It is a very serious matter and one that we must not let slide out of uncertainty.

If anyone has questions as to if someone is suitable for membership, or if there are questions about the fitness of someone joining Masonry, they should contact their Worshipful Master or knowledgeable Masons for advice.

But while joining Freemasonry is not a right of anyone, it should not be denied to anyone who has a desire to join, and is worthy, without a very good cause. Personal disagreements, rumors, jealousy, bigotry, business considerations or any one of countless petty reasons must not guide anyone to deny a good man joining Masonry.

Sadly, because this has seemed to happen more than a few times, some jurisdictions have changed the balloting procedure with some requiring more than one black cube to reject. Abuses do happen. When they do happen, they can forever change attitudes for some.

When we look at a Masonic Lodge, the one officer that truly stands out and is unique in the world of organizations and clubs is the office of Worshipful Master. The authority given to the Master of a Lodge far exceeds the authority given to the presiding officer of any club. This is one of the reasons why the standard edition of *Roberts Rules of Order* is so problematic when used in a lodge. It is also why some years back, I revised the work into a Masonic Edition[1] to make it more suitable for use in the Lodge.

To give just one example, in a club, if the presiding officer rules something out of order, members of the club can call for a vote in an effort to overturn the ruling. If it is overturned, then the ruling of the presiding officer becomes invalid. No such provision exists in Freemasonry. If the Master rules something out of order, that ruling is final. There is no recourse in the Lodge for such a ruling. The idea that Freemasonry is a true democracy is just not correct. If the Master were to make some grievous error or abuse of his authority, then the only recourse would be through the Grand Lodge. In a Lodge setting the decision of the Master is final.

But there are limits to the authority of the Worshipful Master.

The Master does not have the authority to overrule the vote of a Lodge. If the Master believes that a motion is out of order, then he can rule it as such and refuse the call for a vote. But if he does call for a vote, then he also becomes bound to the vote of the Lodge. Once the Lodge has voted his hands are tied. The duties and prerogatives of a Worshipful Master are normally spelled out in Grand Lodge monitors or books of law.

The rules, laws, duties, and prerogatives of a Worshipful Master for your jurisdiction should be read and studied carefully by anyone seeking to work through the chairs of a Lodge.

Another area of Masonic law that is always painful is a Masonic trial. Because Masons are human, we sometimes fail and can violate the trust a Lodge has placed in us.

Each Grand Lodge has rules and regulations concerning Masonic trials. If there is ever a concern that someone has committed a Masonic offense and the possibility of a Masonic trial exists, then you should seek the advice of knowledgeable Masons. The Master or Secretary of the Lodge should be contacted, and, if necessary, contact a District Deputy Grand Master or the office of the Grand Secretary.

A Masonic trial is, without question, nothing that should be taken lightly. You should never threaten Masonic trial during an argument with a brother, nor make bluffs about filing charges on another Mason. If someone has committed an offense serious enough for Masonic trial, then you should begin the process. Don't threaten, just do it. But you should *never* file Masonic charges if no real offense has taken place. You should, however, file Masonic charges if an actual offense has taken place. Not filing Masonic charges, when it *is* warranted, is as bad as filing them when it is not warranted.

But when is something an actual Masonic offense?

In all cases, and this cannot be said enough, *seek the counsel of knowledgeable Masons*. Do not do anything if you are angry or upset. Do not do anything unless you are very sure. Know what the Masonic law is and be sure of every step you take.

If something happens that you believe to be an unjust action, either by individual Masons or, even, Grand Lodge officers, *never, never, never* take your grievances and publicly air them with names and actual cases on social media, or any public platform. Making a public spectacle of perceived flaws in specific Masons or Masonic organizations is the definition of speaking evil. This is *not* how worthy Masons act or solve problems. Any Mason using public soapbox tactics to call attention to perceived flaws in individual Masons or Masonic bodies should be ignored and recognized as unMasonic in his actions.

If you have the unfortunate responsibility of holding office in a Lodge during a Masonic trial you are to pay close attention to your Masonic handbook of law to make sure that everything is done properly. The Master and Secretary of the Lodge should be in close contact with the Grand Secretary's office to make sure that they are doing everything proper and by the rules and regulations of your jurisdiction.

In the case of Masonic trial, there is no such thing as one rule for all, as each jurisdiction will have their own rules and proper conduct for a Masonic trial. Even if a Lodge has never conducted a Masonic trial before, the possibility always exists.

Those seeking to become Worshipful Master of the Lodge should learn and be familiar with how to conduct a trial in the event it would occur. A Masonic trial is not something that an inexperienced or poorly qualified Master would want to tackle on his own.

Seek help, seek guidance, do not act without advice.

Aristotle is said to have written, "At his best, man is the noblest of all animals; separated from law and justice he is the worst." I believe that this is exactly why Freemasonry was created around the concept of very specific rules and laws.

Our obligations are laws, and we agreed to bind ourselves to them under penalty of trial and possible expulsion. We are expected to obey the laws of the land and yet, we can be put on trial for violations of laws that are nowhere to be found in any criminal book of laws for general society. We are held to a higher standard. Why? I believe it is because far more is expected from those who are given far more.

Masonry, I believe, has a vulnerability that exists because of the manner in which we view ourselves, the trust we place in our brothers and the manner in which we write our laws. We don't expect our Brothers to be anything but noble.

As I boy, I remember my grandfather, a Past Master, telling me that he would trust a Mason with anything he had. He said that he would trust a Mason he didn't know in his home alone with all his valuables around. He said that he would trust him *because* he was a Mason. Just a few years ago, I asked a Mason if he would do as my grandfather had done. He smiled and said that there is no way that he would trust *anyone* he didn't know in his home alone with his valuables.

Who is right and who is wrong?

Being a Mason meant something to my grandfather. But what did it mean to him? What does it mean to Masons today? Are we without Masonic law and justice? Is *Masonic jurisprudence* only words that mean *something* that we don't really need to figure out because we have already received our Master Mason degree? Maybe to some.

I have seen a new wave of Masons who seek the deeper aspects of Freemasonry. I see young Masons who want the social clubs to be replaced with true Masonic Lodges. To be so, we need to be noble. We need to know what a "true Masonic Lodge" and a "true Mason" means. We need fair and firm laws, rules and regulations with which to govern our Lodges. We need to have the integrity to uphold our laws and the strength to make sure that all do the same.

My grandfather also told me one other thing. He said that if Masonry were easy, everyone would be a Mason. I believe he was right.

Notes:

1. Poll, Michael R. , Rev. *Robert's Rules of Order: Masonic Edition*. New Orleans, LA: Cornerstone Book Publishers, 2005.

The "Four" Bodies of the Scottish Rite

I wanted to write a few words about something concerning the Supreme Council, Southern Jurisdiction that I have recently heard – but really, it applies to all of the Scottish Rite. It is not truly an error, but is of a nature that it is more along the lines of a misunderstanding that could lead to an error. Let me explain.

Human Beings are interesting creatures. Often times when we are in a group, be it family or close friends, we will talk in what is more of a coded language or abbreviated manner. We will understand perfectly what the other means, but someone from the outside hearing us will have no idea as to what we are talking about. I'll give you an example. The other day I was home doing some work and my wife came into the room with the car keys in her hands. She said, "I'll be back in a minute. I'm going to the store." Well, I knew exactly what she meant, and where she was going. She meant that she was going to a grocery store that is just a couple of blocks away. This same event has happened so many times that she didn't need to further explain where she would be going to deliver the proper and correct information. But if someone from the outside had heard her, what information would they have? They would not know if she meant a grocery store, or drug store, or hardware store, or some other store. All they would know is that she is going out to some store. When we speak in this coded, short cut language, it is usually for those close to us and those who know us well. For others, it can only cause confusion, and the opportunity for misunderstanding is high.

I have recently seen on a few Scottish Rite websites, print media and even on Scottish Rite "official looking" documents and lectures, a certain phrase that I believe can lead to a misunderstanding of the nature of the Scottish Rite. The phrase is, "The Four Bodies of the Scottish Rite." Now, what is being written or spoken about are the four bodies in a local consistory that confer the Scottish Rite degrees from the 4th to the 32nd. These four bodies would be the Lodge of Perfection, Chapter Rose Croix, Council of Kadosh, and the Consistory (some supreme councils may have different names for these bodies). For those Scottish Rite Masons who have been taught the correct nature of the Scottish Rite, they will understand what is meant by this phrase. But new Scottish Rite Masons, or those who have been given no real instruction of the Scottish Rite, might well misunderstand a phrase like this one. Many will actually believe that there are only four bodies in the Scottish Rite.

When we speak of "the Scottish Rite" what we mean may change depending on the conversation. If we are speaking of the degrees of the Scottish Rite that are worked in a local consistory, then we are talking about 29 degrees. If we are speaking about *all* of the degrees of the Scottish Rite, then we are talking about 33 degrees. If we are speaking about the organization of the Scottish Rite, then again, it depends on if we are speaking about a local consistory or the whole of the Scottish Rite. There are four bodies in a local consistory, but six in the

Scottish Rite. We often forget (or don't know) that all 33 degrees of the Scottish Rite exist and are worked in different bodies. The three craft degrees of the Scottish Rite do exist and are worked in craft lodges. The 33rd degree of the Scottish Rite exists and is an actual degree – the final one. It is conferred by the body known as the supreme council.

To believe that there are only 29 degrees, or four bodies, in the Scottish Rite is simply incorrect. The Southern Jurisdiction does not work in the craft ritual of the Scottish Rite, but this does not mean that these degrees, or this Scottish Rite body, does not exist. Under the jurisdiction of the Grand Lodge of Louisiana are ten craft lodges that work in the Scottish Rite craft ritual. They are as much Scottish Rite degrees as any other degree of the Scottish Rite. To believe that regular craft lodges of the AASR do not exist is to simply be wrong. Being uninformed of the truth does not turn fiction into fact.

We also must think of the other end of the spectrum. A supreme council is also a body of the Scottish Rite. In the Southern Jurisdiction, it controls the 33rd degree. In other jurisdictions, other degrees may be controlled by a supreme council. I have heard some Scottish Rite Masons insist that the Scottish Rite works no more than 29 degrees. I was once told this by a brother who was wearing a lapel pin suggesting that he had received the 33rd degree. I asked him if he was a 33rd. He said yes. I then asked him how he could hold the 33rd degree in a system that he claims only works 29 degrees. After stammering a bit, he said that the 33rd degree is an "honorary" degree. I did not take the time to point out that by his logic, the 31st and 32nd degrees would also be "honorary" degrees as it was clear he was both uninformed and determined to believe whatever he wanted.

The 33rd degree is the final degree of the AASR. The degree originally meant that when one received the degree, they would also receive the office of Sovereign Grand Inspector General. The degree and the office were a box set. Just before the time of Albert Pike, the Southern Jurisdiction made a change in how the degree would be conferred. It was decided that the degree would be given to worthy 32nds who would be receiving the degree but *not* the office of Sovereign Grand Inspector General. They would be 33rds, but *Honorary* Sovereign Grand Inspector General or *Honorary Members* of the Supreme Council (rather than *Active Members* who vote in the supreme council). I believe that this is why some confuse the degree with the office and claim the *degree* to be the honorary aspect rather than the office. It's just another reason why education is so important.

Now, if we are at a consistory meeting or with a group of knowledgeable Scottish Rite Masons, then we should be able to speak about the Scottish Rite in any sort of "coded language" as we like. We will understand what we mean and the true nature of the Scottish Rite. But if we are in the presence of young Scottish Rite Masons or those who we know have but limited understanding of the Scottish Rite, then we should be mindful of how we speak. We should not speak in any manner other than that which is perfectly clear so those who hear us will understand exactly what we mean. When misunderstandings happen, they can carry on to later misconceptions and erroneous beliefs by some young Masons who, in later years, may become our leaders.

Our words carry weight. We must be careful of them and always speak and write in as clear a manner as possible so that the actual meaning of whatever we are talking about is properly delivered and received. We must keep in mind that Freemasonry is an educational system. Our job is to teach, not confuse or mislead. When necessary, our job is to also correct misconceptions.

The Scottish Rite is a 33 degree system. It has 33 degrees worked in six different bodies. Its first degree is the Entered Apprentice degree that is worked in the body known as the craft lodge along with the Fellowcraft and Master Mason. In the Southern Jurisdiction, the 4th to the 32nd degrees of the Scottish Rite are worked in a consistory. The 33rd degree is conferred and controlled by the supreme council. Each body controls the degrees that it is entitled to control. The Southern Jurisdiction does not, itself, confer or control the craft degrees of the Scottish Rite. By the same turn, no craft lodge, nor any of the bodies in a consistory, confers the 33rd degree. The Southern Jurisdiction controls, or has under its jurisdiction over, all of the Scottish Rite degrees from the 4th to 33rd. It relinquished jurisdiction over the Scottish Rite craft degrees to the various Grand Lodges in its early days.

I believe that the best way to understand the Scottish Rite is to separate it into two divisions – the ritual and the organization. From a ritual standpoint, it has 33 actual degrees. Period. From an organizational standpoint, the various degrees are conferred in different bodies of the organization which, at times, may mean different jurisdictions. It's not an exactly clear system, and it is why education should be in the forefront of the minds of each valley so that its members will properly understand the nature of this beautiful system.

The New Atlantis and Freemasonry

I'd like to take the opportunity to talk about a few words that I believe are too often misused and misunderstood. I also believe that because these words are misused and misunderstood, it has helped create some of the misinformation about Freemasonry. The words are religion, spirituality, religious, and spiritual.

The terms "religion" and "spirituality" are often understood by some as meaning the same thing, but that "spirituality" is viewed to some as an unacceptable and ungodly form of religion. This is not correct. Both religion and spirituality recognize that there is more to life than earthy existence. Both reach out to that *something more*.

But the endgame of religion and spirituality are different. While both deal with human existence and how one should live their life, religion defines the afterlife and structures its philosophy of living with the end goal of salvation and existence following death. Spirituality seeks only to find a way to live as successful as possible in the physical body.

Spirituality, unless modified, does not deal with the afterlife other than to acknowledge it. As such, spirituality cannot be a religion by how we understand the word. But how do we understand the word "religion"?

Most of us understand the word "religion" to mean a belief system in something beyond human existence. We understand that there are many different religions, each having their own doctrine, rules, and regulations for their particular religious faith.

Belief in the doctrines of a religion but *not proof* of these doctrines is necessary as the very nature of religion contradicts what we understand as proof. We have religious beliefs for reasons deeper than what we can see, touch, or understand. But that's not the only definition of religion.

If I spoke of the *religion* of football, it would certainly seem odd, and maybe it would seem a bit disrespectful of religion, but the phrase would be accurate. Used in that context, I would simply be speaking of the great interest that some have in the game of football. It would be proper according to our language. But such a phrase as the "religion of football" it is rarely used because of the potential to create confusion and the appearance of disrespect to the other understanding of the word. This was exactly how Albert Pike ran into trouble when he spoke of the *religion of Freemasonry*. What he meant was the strong interest that Masons have in Freemasonry. But many anti-Masons twisted his words to mean was that Freemasonry *itself* was a religion. It was exactly the same as Pike's use of the word Lucifer. It was written with one meaning, but understood by some by another.

There is no way that I can enter the mind of Albert Pike and know exactly *why* he used these particular phrases. In my studies of the man, however, it is not impossible that he knew exactly how his words would be misunderstood, and he used them anyway. It's not impossible that he did so for his personal amusement, or a desire to not be limited in how he may properly use a language, regardless of how it is misunderstood. Anyway, this is how we use words and sometimes misunderstand each other.

In religion, the name of the "Supreme Being" varies from faith to faith. Since Freemasonry accepts the worthy from all sincere religions, it uses the blanket term "Grand Architect of the Universe" – or a term very close to that depending on the jurisdiction.

Most religions are not so flexible with their version of how the Supreme Being should be identified, addressed, or defined.

Like religion, spirituality recognizes the existence of "something more" but there is a very important difference in how religions are understood.

In spirituality, the goal is to touch that which is greater than man in order to be able to live a better, more productive, and happy life. The goal of religion is not only to deal with physical existence, but the afterlife. Spirituality does not deal with the afterlife. Its sole purpose is to be of assistance to humanity in the physical life.

Many religions seek salvation so that we may be rewarded following death. Spirituality does not concern itself with what comes after death. It's job is to make human existence as productive and beneficial as possible. Spirituality seeks to understand the meaning of life, and this would include a beneficial and productive existence. It seeks to understand the question of why are we here. Spirituality does not, at all, deny the afterlife, but is only focused on the here and now.

Just as there are many different religious faiths, there are many different concepts of spirituality as well as its goals, purpose, and role in human life. In truth, Spirituality is an element of most religions and this is where problems of misunderstanding may exist — just as the misunderstandings of Freemasonry exist. This misunderstanding comes from the concept of something, or someone, being religious.

For some reason it is perfectly acceptable for an individual to be considered religious. I imagine that this is because an individual is not considered a religion in himself or by himself. But a group of people holding like beliefs could well be considered a religion. This may be why if an organization is considered religious, then some are perfectly content taking the next step by saying that this *organization* is a religion. Maybe this comes from the many Protestant faiths that sprang out of the Roman Catholic Church. If these groups of people could create religions, then why can't others — such as the

Freemasons? The argument is not correct, but it does have an element of logic.

It is here that conspiracy theory comes into play. Freemasonry looks like, acts like, and professes to be a religious organization. Freemasonry has secrets. Freemasonry professes *not* to be a religion. Therefore, Freemasons must be lying and *are* some undesirable religion that they do not wish to admit to being. It's the perfect fodder for conspiracy theory. There is no defense because the charges are not fact-based.

Conspiracy theorists *want* to believe what they believe and choose to see any denial of their charges as willful lying. Facts are not necessary. Because spirituality does contain elements of religion it is also painted with the same brush and denounced by some as an undesirable religion. Those who try to point out that spirituality is not, itself, a religion but only a system designed to help humans better live their lives, are also dismissed as liars.

At some point we must understand that everyone has the right to believe whatever they want to believe. We should not allow ourselves to be dragged down by what others choose to believe or misunderstand. We must go on doing the best we can and understand that others may not understand – either by limitations or choice.

Manly P. Hall is quoted as saying: "Words are vehicles of ideas, and unless they are understood properly misunderstanding is inevitable." It would seem that since words have been used to describe the nature of both religion and spirituality, and words are capable of being misunderstood, then some will always misunderstand the nature of spirituality. If we combine this with those who choose not to understand, then the number of misunderstandings grow even further.

I've read several papers that explore surveys taken concerning religion in America. It seems, at least based on these surveys, that there is an ever-expanding group of Americans who check the "none box" when asked about their religious affiliation. The segment of those who associate themselves with no particular organized religion call themselves "spiritual but not religious." According to these papers, they now constitute at least 20 percent of the US population, and 30 percent of those under 30 years of age.

Is this correct? How do they understand these terms?

Does misunderstanding about labels and terms create misinformation about how these people actually feel? Maybe since these individuals claim to *not* belong to any organized religion, but do claim to be "spiritual" then this can explain how some may feel that spirituality is their religion.

Manly Hall is also quoted as writing: "The true Mason is not creed-bound. He realizes, with the divine illumination of his lodge, that as a Mason his religion must be universal: Christ, Buddha or Mohammed, the name means little, for he recognizes only the light and not the bearer. He worships at every shrine, bows before every altar, whether in temple, mosque or cathedral, realizing with his truer understanding the oneness of all spiritual truth."

It is something to consider.

Some hold a religious belief that Freemasonry is incompatible with their understanding of Christianity. According to how they view Christianity, one is not a *true Christian* if he associates with anyone who is not viewed to be a *true* Christian. Manly Hall tells us that the religion held by a Mason must be universal. Not everyone agrees with that thought. He also quoted as saying that we must embrace those who sincerely seek to be better, yet follow a religious belief different than our own. Very few grand lodges would suggest that this is anything but the truth.

So, by this understanding, Freemasonry would be incompatible with one who believed that they could not associate with anyone who thought or believed differently than themselves. Once again we see that not everyone can or should be a Freemason.

Albert Einstein is quoted as telling us, "Science without religion is lame, religion without science is blind." What does that mean?

In his paper, "The Spiritual Significance of Freemasonry,"[1] Silas Shepherd tells us, "every student of Freemasonry is agreed that its forms and ceremonies are but a means and method of bringing man to a better comprehension of the real purpose of life, and to develop the qualities of his soul." All of these quotes take us in the same direction and that is that at some point we have to decide on a path. And it will be okay if others do not agree with us.

We have to decide *what* we believe, and do so even if we cannot understand why we believe something. If reality exists, then we are going to have to define what reality means to us. It is incumbent upon *us* to determine the nature of our own religious belief, spirituality, and our understanding of these words and how they relate to every aspect of our lives.

We must understand that the Masonic philosophy will not appeal to or be accepted by many, and that this is okay.

C.S. Lewis tells us, "A man can no more diminish God's glory by refusing to worship Him than a lunatic can put out the sun by scribbling the word 'darkness' on the walls of his cell."

Reality exists no matter if we understand it, acknowledge it, or accept it. Reality may also not be the same for everyone. No matter what we want or believe others may disagree with us. Another may have a completely different idea as to the nature of spirituality or religion. Others may unfairly and harshly judge us. But that is their right. No one has the right to physically harm us, but everyone can believe whatever they choose.

Those Freemasons who believe that the nature of Freemasonry should be altered in an attempt to make it universally accepted neither understand the actual nature of Freemasonry nor the folly of their goal. Freemasonry has defined its nature in our rituals, teachings and ceremonies. We are what we are.

In my over forty years of being a Mason, I have found nothing in any of the teachings of Freemasonry that would make me believe that it considers itself, or is in fact, a religion, or anti-religion, or anti-anything other than anti-ignorance.

But by my understanding of the word "religious" I readily admit that Freemasonry is a *religious* organization. I see the Bible on our altars, I see Bible scriptures included in our rituals and ceremonies and I see the same moral teachings that are taught in religions. However, by my understanding of the word, Freemasonry is only a *religious organization*. I do not see any plan of salvation in Freemasonry. The only mention of salvation that I have seen in any Masonic teachings is to refer the Mason to his *own religion*. I have never seen any religion teach that in order to find salvation they would need to seek out *another* religion.

I find it nonsensical to insist that something is a religion when it possesses none of the proper ingredients and does not defined itself as such. Because Freemasonry does seek, through its teachings, to help its members become better human beings and live up to the best of our abilities, I do see Freemasonry as spiritual.

We do acknowledge that there is more to life than physical existence. We do require a belief in a Supreme Being in order to join us, but we do not define or judge another's religion. We do not tell our members that they must belong to this or that religious faith. We simply tell them to use the mind that God has given them and settle matters of religious belief by whatever means is correct *for them*.

In his paper, "The New Atlantis and Freemasonry"[2] A.J.B. Milbourne writes of a book that many consider to be the blueprint of not only Freemasonry and not only the Rosicrucian Order, but also the United States of America. Of course, this line of thinking is all speculation bordering on conspiracy theory, but let's look at it for a moment.

This paper deals with the book "The New Atlantis" written by Francis Bacon. Bacon himself is the subject of considerable mystery and speculation. A number of books have been written on Bacon suggesting that he was everything from the real William Shakespeare to the lead editor of the King James Bible. With more substantial evidence he is reputed to have been one of the founders of the Royal Society of London. He was, without question, a writer, scientist and social leader at the height of the Renaissance. From all accounts Bacon was a man of substance, great intelligence, and a desire for humanity to be *something more*. More than a few suggest that the movement from Operative Freemasonry to Speculative Freemasonry was spearheaded by Bacon himself.

I believe that the spiritual nature of the philosophy of Freemasonry does reach into the heart of everyone receptive and touches something deep within us. I believe that those who are receptive to the philosophy of Freemasonry can be of like mind, and by their own personal actions, create social change.

If one Individual decides for himself that he likes chocolate ice cream and then one by one all of his neighbors decide the same thing this would be their choice. Yes, they may have been inspired by one individual, but it was still their choice. No outside spiritual force made them do anything, unless of course we choose to accept far-fetched mind control conspiracy theories. The very natural process is that if one person likes something and then others agree with him a change in the group will take place.

I believe that the Masonic philosophy is a sound philosophy for humanity, it is not that big of a stretch that many — Freemasons or not — would find such a society acceptable. For example, it would not be some controlling spiritual force that created the desire for the English colonies in America in the late 1700's to seek their freedom, it was simply the common goal of the majority of the people. It was what they individually chose.

The New Atlantis happens to tell us of pretty much the same sort of event. It is no small wonder that many see this book as the blueprint for the creation of the United States of America. The land of freedom — including spiritual and religious freedom

— a land of just laws and the opportunity for each individual to grow to the extents of their personal limits.

So, did Francis Bacon create Freemasonry and then give a blueprint, and marching orders, for Freemasonry to come to the New World and create *The New Atlantis* under the name of the United States of America? I won't even attempt to answer such a question. I will however say that Freemasonry provides a personal blueprint which if followed can help each one of us become a better human being.

If each one of us improves ourselves and becomes better than we are today and this practice is done by all those around us, doesn't society as a whole benefit? We may only be an individual and we may only be able to control ourselves, but it has long been known that like-minded individuals can bring about great social change.

So, did Francis Bacon create a super-secret "invisible college" and did he write a book designed to create the perfect world? Well, speculative Freemasonry was created, it did spread all over the world and the United States was created. But how many of us would say that the United States and the organization of Freemasonry are perfect? We are human beings with all the flaws, failings, and potential of other human beings.

I am of the mind to believe that it doesn't much matter why either Speculative Freemasonry or the United States was created. I do not believe it matters if the United States is the New Atlantis or if Freemasonry is that spiritual tie with the Almighty designed to make our time in the physical body as beneficial as possible.

I do not believe the *why* of the question is as important as what we actually do with the situation. If we view Freemasonry as a moral philosophy designed for self-improvement, then the only question we need to deal with is do we want to take advantage of this philosophy and improve ourselves or not?

It is impossible to reach into the heart and mind of any of our neighbors in an attempt to make them better, but it is not impossible for us to make these changes in ourselves.

Maybe the New Atlantis should not be looked at as anything larger than our own home. Maybe everything about the spiritual nature of Freemasonry, as well as ideas of creating Utopian worlds where everything is good and just, should be looked at more personally. Maybe we should not expect changes in society until we make these changes in ourselves.

There is an old saying, "where there is smoke there's fire." The problem is that sometimes we make mistakes. What we believe to be smoke could be a heavy fog. And yet in areas of religion, we very often accept teachings with no expectation of proving the teachings. So we are put in somewhat of a no-win situation when some look at the spiritual nature of Freemasonry and say that it is a religion — a false, anti-Christian, and ungodly religion. Our attempts to argue such statements with those who have no intention of changing their minds are pointless and a waste of everyone's time. If someone has a religious belief that anything spiritual or Masonic is a false religion, then we have to accept that this is their belief and go on with our life.

For those who understand the true nature of Masonry, they will understand that we seek only harmony between ourselves, our world, and the divine spark within us all.

Notes:

1. Shepherd, Silas. "The Spiritual Significance of Freemasonry." *Masonic Enlightenment: The Philosophy, History and Wisdom of Freemasonry*. Ed. Michael R. Poll. New Orleans, LA: Cornerstone Book Publishers, 2006. pp 139-142.

2. Milbourne, A.J.B. "The New Atlantis and Freemasonry." *Masonic Enlightenment: The Philosophy, History and Wisdom of Freemasonry*. Ed. Michael R. Poll. New Orleans, LA: Cornerstone Book Publishers, 2006. pp 151-154.

Words to the New Mason

I believe that the time just before and just after receiving the Blue Lodge degrees is a critical time and information not provided during this time can present problems for any new Mason. Please allow me to share some thoughts with you.

I'd like to first say a few words to the candidates looking to join Freemasonry. What you have done and are doing will lead you to a larger world. But no, if you have read that joining Freemasonry will give you the powers of a Jedi or you will share in the secret wealth of the world, you fell for some nonsense. Freemasonry will give you none of that. At least, Freemasonry will give you none of that if you understand *wealth* to mean money. But if you truly study the teachings of Freemasonry, you can receive a wealth far more important to the wise individual. Freemasonry can give you the keys to unlocking parts within you that can lead you to a spiritually rich, better life. By putting the teachings of Freemasonry into practice you can become a better human being. The Masonic rituals and teachings can unlock doors for you all designed to help you become better than you are today. But unlocked doors will mean nothing unless you take the steps necessary to walk into the room.

If you are someone who has yet to receive his first degree, there are a few things I'd like to talk to you about. If you're waiting for your initiation, this means that you have been balloted upon and you have passed the ballot. All the members of your future lodge who were present voted on you and desire you to be a part of their Lodge — their family. Masons call each other "brothers," and we do so because we are considered family. But it's the act of balloting that I'd like to speak about for a moment. Freemasonry is often said to be tied to the Ancient Mystery Schools through initiation. The craft lodge will provide you with three initiations which can be looked on as the keys to opening those doors that I just spoke about. There is an old thought about initiation that I would like to pass on. The thought is that for initiation to be considered valid three elements must be present. One is the desire to be initiated, the second is the desire to initiate, and the third is the proper setting. The desire for your being initiated was satisfied when you submitted your petition. Freemasonry insists that no one should be talked into joining Masonry, but they must come of their own free will. For initiation to be valid there must be a clear desire to be initiated. The desire to initiate was satisfied with your ballot.

The third element of the successful initiation is really several parts. The proper setting is the Lodge room, or in other organizations which initiate, whatever room is designated as the initiation room. During an initiation, there should be no horse play, laughter, joking around or anything else that can take away from the extremely serious event that is taking place. All present, including you — the candidate — should have an open and clear mind. Should anyone in the Lodge, through carelessness or ignorance, break the solemn mood of the initiation, dismiss them and ignore them. You can control no one else, but you can control yourself. No one is there to make fun of you, use you as a source of entertainment, harass you, or do anything other than offer you the opportunity, through initiation, to open the door to a possible more rewarding life. It is enough for you to know that initiation is far older than Freemasonry and older than most societies. By having a peaceful mind, being as aware as possible and staying open to your feelings, you increase the chances of the initiation being a deeply moving memory that you will carry with you all of your life.

As for technical points, I suggest that you find out the type of Lodge that you are joining before your first initiation. When I say the type of Lodge, I mean if it is a more formal Lodge or one that is more casual in nature. Some Lodges are far more into ritual and education into the various aspects of Masonic symbolism than other Lodges. These types of Lodges usually dress in dark or business suits. If you are unsure, ask ahead of time how you should dress for your initiation. Showing that you care about details may mean a lot.

After your first initiation, you will normally be assigned to an instructor to learn the ritual work expected by your jurisdiction. But this is something that can vary depending on the jurisdiction. In some jurisdictions, new initiates are assigned to a class of instruction. In such classes, students may be assigned instructors on a lasting, or temporary, basis. Whatever the practice is for your jurisdiction, do the work. It is not a waste of your time, nor is it unnecessary busywork. There is an old thought that whatever comes your way free and easy is worth what you paid for it. In the old schools of initiation, payment was *always* necessary for anything one received by means of initiation. Payment may not have been made in actual money, but work was required. It made the initiate realize that what they were receiving was of value. I suggest that you set aside at least a few hours a week for your Masonic study, more of possible. Meet with your instructor, or instructors, as often as possible. Listen to them, do what they ask, and in the very beginning, try to temper any possible enthusiasm you have and limit your questions and actions to what is asked of you. There will come a time and place for all of your questions.

The actual examination of the candidates and what is expected of them varies from jurisdiction to jurisdiction. If you are sincere in joining Masonry, do what is asked of you. Spend the time necessary to learn the work. If situations in your life unexpectedly change and you simply cannot make the time to do the work necessary to advance, make this change in your situation known to your instructors. Most jurisdictions have time limits on completing your work. But if the situation changes for a candidate making it impossible for them to learn their work, it is rare that this will be held against the candidate. Your family and work come before the Lodge and should be given first consideration. Time for Masonry may come at a later date.

I believe it's best that while one is an Entered Apprentice, or Fellowcraft, they should hold most of the questions about Freemasonry, save aspects of their degrees needed for advancement, and keep general information about the history and philosophy of Freemasonry on hold until their work is complete. I believe that their total focus should be on the work given them. But once a candidate receives the Master Mason degree, no question about the Blue Lodge should be held back. If answers to questions cannot be found in your Lodge, seek them elsewhere. The goal of a new Master Mason is to learn as much as possible about the craft, its reason for existing, its practices as well as its history and philosophy. But a warning, be careful with the internet. So much out there is just outright wrong. In addition, if you ask questions about pretty much anything concerning your lodge on the internet, you may get answers back from very experienced Masons who will be giving you answers that are perfectly correct for their jurisdiction, but completely wrong for yours.

I also suggest paying close attention to the working of your Lodge. If you jurisdiction has been wise enough to change back the alterations of the early to mid-1800s restricting Lodge business to only Master Masons, and your jurisdiction has gone back to the original practice of allowing Entered Apprentices in your business meetings, then your study of Lodge operation should have begun earlier. Watch carefully how business is done in the Lodge. Watch the actions of each of the officers, how they conduct themselves and interact with the membership. Visit the Lodges in your jurisdiction, preferably in your own area. Learn the meeting dates of the Lodges near you. Attend whenever possible. Read as much as you can on Freemasonry. A good encyclopedia or dictionary of Freemasonry is always helpful.

Mackey's Encyclopedia of Freemasonry is considered a classic. The original editions are long out of print but can often be found in used bookstores. Reprints can easily be found.[1] Research societies and lodges are highly recommended. Most jurisdictions have state research lodges and national research lodges such as the Philalethes[2] and the Masonic Society[3] can provide much useful information in the United States.

There is a danger, however, if you are new Mason and you happen to have joined a Lodge that is struggling with membership. The danger is that new Masons will often be grabbed and put into leadership positions before they even know exactly what goes into opening of closing a Lodge. Be careful of that and do not be afraid to say no. I believe it far better to wait a while and seek taking office after a few years of seasoning.

Be also careful of those who seek titles. We are not Freemasons in order to gain power, status, or glory. We are Freemasons in order to gain enlightenment and learn how to better live in this world with our fellow human beings. Power seekers or brokers have no place in Masonry and if or when you encounter them, have nothing to do with them.

This one thing that you should always remember, we represent Freemasonry to the world. Our actions, good or bad, will be how Freemasonry itself is viewed. Do not go out in the world and disrespect either yourself or Freemasonry. Your conduct outside of the Lodge, especially in public is to be of a nature that will a credit Freemasonry and not a disgrace.

Notes:

1. Mackey, Albert. *Mackey's Encyclopedia of Freemasonry*. New Orleans, LA: Cornerstone Book Publishers. Reprint, 2015.

2. http://www.freemasonry.org/

3. http://themasonicsociety.com/

We Need Someone to Speak!

There have been a good number of papers providing sound reasons for bringing speakers into your Lodge, valley or other Masonic bodies to give educational lectures. But I realize that there is a difference between knowing what to do and all that might go into actually doing it. I'd like to talk a little about some of the successes and failures when dealing with Masonic speakers.

As with everything we do in Masonry, planning is of utmost importance. Invariably, when you don't plan things out, whatever can go wrong, will go wrong. Murphy's Law does love Worshipful Masters who believe that everything will just work itself out. Let's look at two general types of events that take place in a Lodge — recurring events and called events. Of course, within each of these two types of events, there is another subgroup of events — public or tiled events. We will talk more about these aspects later. A recurring event happens every year or on a regular basis. Examples are Past Master's Night or the Lodge's birthday. A "called event" is something that is planned to be a one-time event. An example would be if the Worshipful Master decides that he would like to have a speaker give an educational talk on the second meeting in July.

A recurring event may, depending on the event, limit the suitable lecture subjects that may be given in the Lodge. For example, if it is your Lodge's birthday, then a talk on the history of the Scottish Rite or the Shriner's might not exactly fit in with your Lodge's birthday. It would be better to have a talk on the history of your Lodge or Masons in your Lodge who played important roles, or something along this nature. You will want the theme of the event to match up with the talk delivered. If, however, the regular event is a yearly lecture itself with a noted speaker, then it would be appropriate for the lecture to be on whatever subject the lecturer desires.

The point of trying to match an event with a speaker is that many times if you bring in a known speaker, you want to give him every opportunity to shine. Speakers are very often known for their work in specific areas of Freemasonry. If, for example, a speaker is a high ranking York Rite Mason who has given quite a number of highly regarded York Rite lecturers you want to put him to best use. If you bring him in for Eastern Star Appreciation Night, well, he might not give as inspiring a talk on the Eastern Star as he would have on the York Rite. If the speaker does not shine, the Lodge and the WM (for bringing him in) does not shine. Again, this all goes to planning out events and giving them some thought.

When you are planning for a speaker to visit your Lodge, a good time frame is to contact them at least 6 - 8 months in advance. If you are a Junior or Senior Warden and you are planning out your year as WM (which you should do), it is fine to plan on this or that date to have an event where you will have a speaker. It is usually not best, however, to contact and nail down a speaker several years in advance. The exception is if you want to have a popular, nationally known speaker who gives many lectures during the year. In such a case, you very well may need to contact and book him a year or so before the event. You may also need to be a bit flexible with the date for an event. Moving the date of an event, even just until the next meeting or following month, may make all the difference in your being able to secure a well-known speaker. If you wait until a month before an event, you may end up doing the talk yourself.

When planning for a speaker, you must also realize that it is a bit of a different procedure to acquire a local speaker than a national one. A local speaker is one who would be able to drive home after the event with no more than about a half hour to an hour drive. For anyone who comes in from a greater distance, you should plan to make accommodations available for them to spend the night somewhere. Treat both local or out of town speakers the same — with considerable gratitude. They are both helping you out and deserve all consideration.

When you bring in a speaker from out of town, you need to consider hotel arrangements and travel. When setting up a hotel for your speaker, you want to select a nice hotel as near as possible to your Lodge (or wherever the event will take place), but you do not need to break the bank by selecting the most expensive hotel. You certainly do not want to put your speaker in a budget hotel, but a nice, upper/mid-range hotel not far from the event shows that you care. When setting up the hotel room, you will need to know if the speaker needs any special accommodations, such as electronic connections, etc. You will also need to know if they are bring someone or coming alone. You need to find out all details of what they need for a successful and pleasant stay. You want everything ready for the speaker so that all they need do is show up at the hotel and everything will be ready and paid for them.

Travel can be a little more complicated. If someone is flying in, how you pay their airfare may vary depending on the location and time. Security has become a greater issue than in the past. It is sometimes required that passengers pay for their own tickets out of security concerns. If this is the case, then you should try to make the payment as easy as possible for the speaker. If you can learn the cost of the ticket, send the speaker a check for the ticket ahead of time so that he can purchase it without any out of pocket costs. If the speaker does pay for the ticket, reimburse him immediately. The speaker should not be inconvenienced because he has agreed to do you a favor.

If the speaker is coming in by car, you want to know the distance the speaker is traveling so that you can cover his mileage. If the speaker is coming enough of a distance that he will need to stay overnight somewhere before arriving, you also want to cover any hotel expenses necessary. You want to make the whole experience for the speaker as easy and convenient as possible. If they are coming by bus or train, then the same thing applies. If at all possible, have it so that all they need do is pick up their ticket at the depot or where ever is necessary. If it is not possible to pre-pay the ticket for them, send them the funds ahead of time or reimburse them immediately.

Speakers should also not be required to find their way from the airport or terminal to their hotel. Someone should be available to pick up the speaker when he arrives, take him to his hotel, and then drive him to the location of the event. If he arrives early in the day, have someone available to take him out to lunch and, if he is willing, show him around to see some sights. Of course, some speakers like to prepare for their talk, so play everything by ear. The point is that you do not want to just deposit the speaker and leave him on his own to fend for himself unless this is his desire. It is important to stay in touch with the speaker while he is on his way to the event. Try to cover every detail, schedule and plan with the speaker so that everyone will be on the same page.

When you set up an event with a speaker, the thing that everyone wants is as few bad surprises as possible. You want to take care of everything for the speaker so that he has no issues and minimize the chance of problems. One suggestion to keep surprises to a minimum is to stay in touch with the speaker. If you make all the arraignments six months in advance, you will want to contact him a few times over the next few months to make sure all is well. You certainly want to be in touch with him more than a few times during the month of the event as this will be the time when you are setting up the travel and hotel reservations.

I know of one case where a speaker was secured a good six months before an event. But the Worshipful Master did not again contact him again once all the plans had been finalized. As it turns out, the speaker had a serious heart attack two weeks before the lecture date. Because the Worshipful Master had not contacted him, he knew nothing about the heart attack. The speaker was in the hospital recovering from surgery and certainly not thinking about anything else. The Master simply assumed that all was well and when the speaker did not show up at the Lodge that night, they were caught without a speaker. If the Worshipful Master had been in touch with him two weeks or even one week before the event, he would have had time to make some sort of "plan B" and not have everyone waiting for a talk that would not happen.

Things can happen to anyone at any time. A wise Worshipful Master will always have back-up plans. He will keep in touch with speakers so that he can minimize any surprise event so that the damage will be minimal. If you plan for nothing and just wait for an event to happen, the worst can and sometimes does happen. The Master and the Lodge will ultimately be the ones to look bad.

You will want the phone number of the speaker, and you will want to keep in touch with him even after he is on his way to your area. Make sure all is going well, ask if he needs anything, and make sure he has your phone number and the number of at least one other person. Keeping in touch is a must.

There are a number of possibilities as to the format and venue of an event itself. It can be public or tiled, at the Lodge or at another location. It can be a dinner lecture or a lecture with the audience in rows of chairs.

Let's talk about if the lecture for the evening will be public or in a tiled Lodge, or another location that is tiled. It may seem unnecessary to say, but you need to tell the speaker at the very beginning if his talk will be public or for Masons only. I well remember one speaker coming to a lodge fully expecting his talk to be in a tiled Lodge with Masons only in attendance. His talk concerned a good number of aspects of Masonic ritual. He was shocked when he arrived and saw that family and friends (non-Masons) were in attendance. The Master had not told him that it would be a public event. It was a horrible talk as he had to edit it on the fly, leaving out most of the obvious important sections. When you don't communicate with the speaker, you get surprises.

And then there are dinner lectures. I remember one lecture that I was invited to give many years ago. The event was held at a country club, and I knew in advance that it would be a public lecture. It was a truly beautiful place. The waiters brought around the salads first. It was wonderful. After a short time, they brought the main course – a beautiful prime rib plate. Then the surprise came. No sooner than the waiter put my plate in front of me did the Master get up and introduce me to speak. I had not even taken a single bite. I got up and looked at everyone eating in front of me. I then looked at my plate of food and knew full well that it would be stone cold by the time I finished the lecture. I was shocked and not at all happy at the obvious lack of consideration they had given me. My solution was to thank them all for the invite and the wonderful meal that was sitting there getting cold while I was talking. I cut the lecture down *quite* a bit and then sat down to eat my meal while it was still reasonably hot. The moral of this story is that if you have a dinner lecture, make sure that the lecture is *before* or *after* the meal, not *during*. It should be obvious, but clearly it is not always.

Find out if the speaker needs any special audio/video equipment or connections. Some speakers like to use slides, others have computer animated shows. Find out exactly what the speaker needs and let him know with what you can provide him. If you can't do something that he wants, let him know so that he can make other plans for the lecture. Also, let him know if you have a podium available and the mic system. Some Lodges have horrible acoustics and if someone is giving a lecture and the ones in the back can't hear him, it is a bad surprise.

If the lecture is going to be in a tiled Lodge and it is a regular meeting with business, take special care with how you acknowledge and deal with the speaker. I saw a Lodge bring in an out of town speaker and when the Lodge opened, the Master did not even acknowledge the speaker. He went straight to the regular business, minutes and bills with not a single word about the speaker. Clearly, he had the meeting planned out and the speaker was to fall in a certain slot. When all of the business was finished, he simply said that it was time for the speaker and invited him up to talk. I believe the whole event happened the way it did because the Master was simply not prepared or knowledgeable about how to accommodate visitors. I do not believe that his intention was to ignore the speaker or make him feel that his talk was not really all that important, but that is certainly how it seemed.

When a speaker comes to your Lodge, make it very clear and obvious that you are very appreciative that he came. As soon as you open the Lodge, receive him as you would any dignitary and have a few prepared words of thanks for him. Let him know that you are grateful he came. Invite him to sit in the East with you. It is not necessary to put off any business of the Lodge once you have properly acknowledged the speaker, but make it perfectly clear that you are happy he is there with you and that his presentation is important to all.

There is also a sometimes delicate (or completely ignored or forgotten) subject that I would like to discuss. While paying all the travel and accommodations for a speaker is generally understood, there is the subject of an honorarium. A speaker who provides an educational talk for a Lodge is providing a valuable service. He is also taking his time off from doing other things to provide this service to your Lodge because you asked him. For out of town lectures, he is likely committing several days to helping you. It is only fair that he be reimbursed for his efforts and time. Many times this is something that is completely ignored by a Lodge. My own belief is that it is something that just is not considered or realized. During my Masonic life, I have given many, many lectures and yet I can count on my hand the number of times that I have received an honorarium. I believe that in my case, as well as with many other speakers, it simply feels awkward and inappropriate to have to ask about an honorarium. Like many other Masonic authors, I normally bring books to sell to members, but not always. It is a delicate matter and most speakers feel uncomfortable asking for something that should not have to be spoken about. It feels like begging. On the other hand, I know several Masonic speakers who are very upfront with the fact that their time is valuable and if a Lodge or other Masonic body wants an event, then this is their speaking fee. The average honorarium is two to five hundred dollars, depending on the financial standing of the Lodge. I have seen more than one "less than rich" Lodge passing the hat for a speaker with everyone being as generous as they could for the educational opportunity. Most Masonic speakers will provide lectures even if nothing at all above the travel and hotel expense is offered. They do so because they care about Masonic education. The point is that if a Lodge can, they should help the one who is helping them. As with everything else, discuss any honorarium when you first contact a speaker so that he is aware of what your Lodge will offer. Don't make them ask.

One other situation needs to be discussed. It is when a Masonic author contacts a Lodge informing them of certain dates he will be in your town promoting a new Masonic book that he has released. The author may offer to deliver a talk to your Lodge and make available his book for sale to the members. There is not a thing in the world wrong with this, and it offers the opportunity for the Lodge to have an easy event that is pretty much only in need of settling on a date. The Lodge needs not make hotel or travel accommodations available for the speaker as the speaker was coming to town anyway on a promotion of his book. The same is true of an honorarium. In this case, it is unnecessary as the author/speaker will be initiating the event. All that is necessary is to find out what the author needs and what you have available. Let him know if you plan a public or tiled event.

Masonic Lodges are designed to educate its members. Inviting a speaker to your Lodge is a significant part of that Masonic education. Don't treat it as something less than a very important event. Make your plans early. Cover all details so that the Lodge and the speaker know exactly what will happen — how, when and where. If you follow the steps in this paper, you can have a far better chance of an outstanding event.

The Role of Music in Freemasonry

Pythagoras is said to have written: "There is Geometry in the humming of the strings, there is music in the spacing of the spheres." Let's try to explore this subject just a bit.

I joined Freemasonry in the mid-1970s. My Lodge was located in downtown New Orleans in the old Masonic Temple building. The Lodge met in one of the large, old Lodge rooms in the building. In the north of the room was a fairly large, dusty pipe organ. No one in the Lodge played it, and once when I tried to turn it on, it just made a hissing sound. It clearly had been unused for many years. I asked one of the older members about it, and they told me stories of how many years prior an organist would play during every degree, and also during the meetings. He said that when he died, no one knew how to play the organ, and it just fell into disuse.

Over the years, I've thought about the role of music in Freemasonry. Of course, I read about the classical musicians such as Mozart, Haydn and others who were Freemasons and also more or less modern Masonic composers such as John Philip Sousa. I also noted music as one of the seven liberal arts and sciences referred to in our Masonic teachings. I've even found collections of Masonic sheet music written by Masons in the 1800s. Clearly, music was a significant part of the Masonic Lodge experience prior to my time of joining.

Over time, and like so many other aspects of the Masonic Lodge experience, music in the Lodge seems to have all but faded away. Today, I see very few lodges with either a piano or organ in the Lodge room. I have, however, seen degrees conferred with musicians playing acoustic guitar or saxophone with appropriate music. These degrees stand out with me as the more impressive degrees that I have witnessed.

I have also seen a few lodges who use a CD with appropriate Masonic music. Clearly there was a desire for music during a degree, but no musicians were available. I give these lodges an "A" for effort, but the canned music was always lacking some due to problems with the speakers or other electronic issues. In my opinion, live music with a competent musician is always the best experience.

But when did music become a part of the Masonic initiation experience?

As music was included in the seven liberal arts and sciences, clearly our appreciation for music was always present, but did it play a part in the actual work of the old operative Freemasons? I tend to doubt so, at least as far as their actual construction work.

Let's think about this for a minute. Today, if you go to any building site you might well hear music coming from a boombox for the entertainment of the workers. But in the days of the old operatives, in order for the workers to listen to music, actual musicians would have had to been there to play for them. That doesn't seem at all practical. And, I see no record of musicians playing for the workers.

It is very possible that in the evenings, after their work was completed, musicians played for the old operative's enjoyment or possibly during some initiation ceremonies, but again, I've read no account of this happening.

I also believe it possible that the mathematical concepts of music were employed in the training of the old operatives. This would likely have been in association with making them a highly skilled and fully rounded artisan.

But music can also be used to create an atmosphere suitable for the mind and spirit to be ready for the influences of initiations. These are two different applications of music.

Where I do see records of music taking place, in most all aspects of the Masonic experience, is in the very early days of Speculative Freemasonry. I believe that it is very possible that with the shift from Operative to Speculative Freemasonry, music moved from the realm of academic appreciation to one of actual musical performances.

Look at the setting that is recorded for many of the early English speculative lodges. They were located in taverns. Certainly music was played in most all taverns. Soon after Speculative Freemasonry debuted in England, it moved to France. It was here that I believe another change took place or, began taking place.

Once Freemasonry moved from England to France there are several points of logic that we need to consider. One is language and the other is culture. England and France have different languages as well as different cultures. In order for Freemasonry to become widely accepted in France, which it did, it was necessary for the ritual to be translated into French. We have no idea who did it, but clearly *someone* did the translation. And when this translation was written, consideration for the French culture was included.

The French Masonic ritual was clearly written with the *French* in mind. All anyone has to do is witness any Masonic degree from England and one from France and you can see the different cultures represented in how the Masonic work is presented.

Just as the Masonic ritual was crafted for the different cultures so was Masonic music. If we look at what's generally classified as Masonic music, we can see two styles of music that are most prevalent.

One is more meditative in nature and the other uplifting. I don't think of meditative music when I think of an English tavern. I believe that the more meditative music came from other influences. As time passed, the musical influences grew wherever Freemasonry existed. Like so many things, music in

Masonry evolved into what it became by means of the influence of more than one source and over more than a few years.

Clearly music was always a part of the total Masonic educational experience. But it seems to have taken on a new role with the advent of Speculative Freemasonry. Music seems to have evolved from a passive appreciation to an active part of Masonic initiation. Without question, music, and I mean appropriate music, can touch the heart and soul and put any candidate in the proper frame of mind for initiation.

It seems that music was introduced into the Speculative Masonic experience by the English and possibly fine-tuned with the assistance of the French and others. In not too long a time, Masonic initiation was viewed as incomplete without appropriate music setting the tone for the initiation — or, other aspects of the lodge experience.

The loss of Masonic music during Masonic initiations is, in my opinion, a loss for all Freemasonry. I won't suggest that initiation cannot be considered valid without appropriate music, but I will say that a valid initiation that includes music is a far more rich and rewarding experience.

As Lodges move towards a rediscovering of what made Masonic initiation so deeply moving for so many, I believe we need to re-examine the role of music in Freemasonry. I feel that effort should be made to reintroduce music into all aspects of the Masonic Lodge experience.

If we have no musicians available, we can turn to electronics. But if we make the effort, and then keep the effort moving, then step-by-step we can, achieve our goals. Offering music in our lodges is something that every Lodge should consider.

The Cause and Effect of Freemasonry

One of the professed goals of Freemasonry is enlightenment. Masons are said to seek light. But, what is light? Most say that light is knowledge. But knowledge of what? Freemasonry also professes to take good men and make them better. Maybe that gives us a hint. Maybe enlightenment, or knowledge, is designed to give us a better awareness ... of us.

Maybe we improve ourselves by first knowing and understanding ourselves a little better. Once we are better aware of ourselves, or evaluate ourselves, then we are in a position to make improvements in ourselves.

Let's look at a baseball team. If all the members of that team practice hard and improve themselves physically and mentally then, as a whole, the team performs better. But if the members of the team decide that they would rather go out to a party than practice, then it's logical that the performance of the team will suffer. The individual efforts, or lack of efforts, will affect the whole team.

The same is true of the Lodge or any organization in Freemasonry. If all of the members are working together to improve themselves, then they have a direction and the organization as a whole moves in the direction of the teachings – or, if you will, the training. But if there is no personal education, no guidance, no seeking of light, then each individual may be viewed as walking aimlessly.

A Lodge filled with such unenlightened brothers, having no direction, no idea of what to seek or do, is not living up to anyone's full potential. It is a Masonic Lodge of no value. When there are no designs upon the Trestleboard, we can only expect confusion in the Temple.

Sadly, we can grow accustomed to this half-life in Freemasonry and believe that this is all that can be expected. We accept the limitations and structure Masonic activity based on what is, rather than what could be. As human beings, we are very good at making the best out of whatever situation we have. But let's see if we can find some Masonic direction and improve our situations.

OK, let's look for a minute at who we are. We are Freemasons, but we need to qualify that statement. Unless it happens to be our profession, we don't build things for a living. We are what is known as *Speculative Freemasons*. Our work and construction is designed to be internal, inside us. Our work is to make ourselves better.

As far as training ... well, exercise certainly helps everyone, but we do not do physical training in Masonry the same way that physical training is done for, say, a member of a sports team. But, this does not mean that we do no training at all.

If we are serious about what we profess to do in Freemasonry, then it is necessary that we train our minds and gain experience in Lodge operation and the fundamental teachings of our Order. And, just like a sports team, we can do this work ... or not. We have a choice.

But in fairness, it's really not as simple as that. A baseball team does not train in the same way that a basketball team trains or a hockey team trains. Each has their own set of skills that need to be learned and perfected. It would be of very little help to hand someone who knows nothing of hockey, a hockey stick and then tell them that they are a hockey player and that they will have a game next week. It is the same as handing a new

Mason a white apron and telling him that he is a Freemason and then offer him an office in Lodge.

Just like members of a sports team, young Freemasons need a coach. They need to have someone there to show them what to do, let them know where they are going wrong, and guide them so that they can perfect their skills. And I mean *after* they receive the Master Mason degree, not just while they are memorizing a collection of words.

What kind of baseball team owner would gather together a group of people and without any training or coaching at all, put them out to play against a trained team? How could we expect them to be anything but unable to do what we think they should be able to do? It's the same for Masonry.

At some point, and it really serves no good purpose to try and point fingers or blame anyone from the past, but Masonic training did fall by the wayside. Masonic teaching and training in Lodge was replaced by ... well, nothing. We just began making Masons and then, with nothing else, putting them in various offices. Lodge was a place to just visit with friends.

The Lodges adjusted to leaders having little to no education in Masonry. Soon, the leaders were unable to provide to others what was not provided to them. The reason for going to Lodge evolved into supporting a social club with a mystical sounding history. We read minutes, pay bills, talk of who is sick or has died, and that's about it.

And yet, we try to impress others with a mysterious past. This has become the norm. Sincere, well-meaning Masons truly believed that this was the true Masonic Lodge experience. It was a foolish plan and bad fix for something that was broken.

There are several old sayings that I have always found of value. One is that it is better that a thousand worthy men be turned away than one unworthy foot cross the threshold of the Lodge. The other is that to believe that joining a Masonic Lodge makes one a Freemason is the same as believing that joining a music club makes one a musician. We can find great truth in these thoughts.

Not everyone can or should be a Freemason. But, it seems that was then, and this is now. We sometimes find that the only necessary qualification for membership is the funds to pay for the initiation. Some men who never should have joined Masonry, have joined. In fact, more than a comfortable number of these individuals have not only joined, but have risen in leadership in Lodges and even Grand Lodges. Elections come every year and when the pool of qualified candidates dries up, then what is to be done?

So ... we have a situation where good men join Masonry and learn nothing of what should have been taught them. They are unqualified. In addition, some who should never have joined are now members. They are unworthy. Both have learned nothing in the way of Masonic education. Can you begin to see the problem developing? So, what do we do? It's too late for cries of, "We need to better guard the West Gate!"

Let's try to look objectively at the situation.

We are at a point where very few, if any, fail to realize that a problem exists. Some of those who should not ever have joined Masonry have built for themselves little kingdoms in various bodies. These little kingdoms exist to feed their own personal ego and serve as a power base to assure control of "their turf." Others, with good intentions, but who don't completely understand the teachings of Masonry are unable to guide us out of trouble because they lack the ability. These are some of our leaders. Most want to do good, but too many of them are just over their heads. They feel overwhelmed and confused.

But there is another, newer, group and they are worthy of special attention. Over the last dozen or so years, young Masons have been joining with a true hunger and desire to learn the deeper aspects of Freemasonry.

Over the years, commercial books and movies by Dan Brown, and others, made Freemasonry a very popular topic in general society. Many of the young Masons of today joined with a greater knowledge of our teachings than Masons who have been around for many years. In fact, some brand new Masons have a better knowledge of the Masonic philosophy than some of those who have risen to the highest ranks in our Grand Lodges.

We are not in good shape, but we're not without hope.

I believe the answer that we have is contained within our own teachings. Regardless of your own personal level of Masonic education, stop for a moment and think. Think about the lesson of Hiram.

Think of the integrity and courage that he displayed. There is a message there for all of us today. It's not enough that we want to do good, we have to do it. To believe that we do not have the power, authority or ability to make changes is simply not true.

The best way to destroy any organization is to divide its membership. Let's take Freemasonry and reduce it down to its most basic level. We are Freemasons. That's what we are, and how we should identify ourselves. If we identify ourselves as Scottish Rite or York Rite or this or that Lodge or jurisdiction or by any sub-group of Freemasonry, we are only building barriers. We are separating ourselves from our brothers. We are creating a "them and us" situation. It then becomes easy to say that the "other guys" are the reason for all our problems or that if we could only bend the "other guys" to our will, subjugate them, or turn them into us, then all would be well. It's nonsense.

Everyone has their own tastes, preferences, and personal desires. That's our right. Everyone does not have to think, act, or look the same. There is strength in diversity. We need to be confident enough in ourselves to recognize that it's okay if we all do not think alike or have the same opinions on just about anything. It's okay if I want a Masonic body to go in this direction and someone else wants another direction. The problems come when some do not realize that it's okay and object to anything, but what *they* want. They become unreasonable.

When one demands that another do something that is impossible for them, then a barrier is created and the situation becomes impossible. This is not a problem created by Freemasonry. It is a problem created by ignorance of Freemasonry. Still, it's our problem and our responsibility to solve.

If a problem is born out of ignorance, then education would seem to be the answer. We must all move in harmony. We must respect ourselves and others, we must be Freemasons and know the nature of Freemasonry.

If a baseball team goes out on the field and one of the players is dressed to play football with the belief and goal of playing football, then you have a problem. You are playing baseball, not football. It's okay if one member of the team believes that he can't wash his socks out of a belief of good luck, or if another has a "lucky bat" that he always wants to use. All of these things are personal choices and is the right and privilege of each player, as long as they play baseball.

All will be good as long as they work as a team to play the very best game of baseball that is possible for them. But if you come to a baseball game intending on playing another game, then the whole team suffers. Maybe it is the teams fault if they hired you knowing that you were a football player and knew nothing of baseball. But the end result is the same.

If you are a baseball team, you need baseball players. The team has to teach and train you. You have to be willing to put in the time to learn. If this does not happen, then you can't remain on the team. You may be the nicest guy in the world, but if you can't play baseball, then you can't be on a baseball team. If you don't know Freemasonry, then you need to either learn or remain on the sidelines. If we try to bend Masonry to the point that it becomes something else, well then it will be something else. We have to recognize that fact.

One of the basic Masonic teachings that I feel we need to understand is respect. We need to respect ourselves, others and the Lodge — or, whatever Masonic body we are in. Respect comes from kind feelings, appreciation, fairness and compassion – but also strength. When we receive these feelings, it makes us feel good. Others feel good when they receive these feelings from us. Everyone benefits.

We need to recognize that everyone has the right to feel good, be respected, and be a part of the whole. When "the other guy" is not respected, we pull apart, throw up protective shields, and the whole organization becomes fractured and of little to no benefit to anyone.

The lesson of Hiram is designed to teach us the importance of integrity and courage. He could have made the ruthless craftsmen happy by giving them what they wanted. But he knew that it was not right. He did not show them disrespect, but he also would not allow them to take away the respect that was due him as well as the organization to which they all belonged.

When he realized that they were at an impasse and that the only way to accommodate them was by casting away everything in which he believed, as well as violating his word, his honor and his integrity, then he just stopped. He would no longer participate in what they wanted. Whatever they were going to do was up to them, but he would not allow them to take him down a path that he knew was wrong. He did not yell or scream or cause any sort of disturbance, he simply stopped participating.

We cannot get around the simple law of cause and effect. What we do has a consequence. What we don't do has a consequence. Too many times we know in our heart what is right and what is wrong, but we fail to take action because we fear doing damage or upsetting others with our actions. Truly, that helps no one. It shows respect for no one.

Look, if you are lost in the woods and going North is only taking you deeper in, turn around. Don't let pride or ego keep you on a path that is not helping you. If you participate in activities that you know are going in the wrong direction, then I assure you, whatever you may tell yourself, you become part of the problem not the solution.

Esoteric Initiation

Freemasonry is an Initiatic Order. This means that we initiate candidates into membership. We can find many examples of initiation in numerous ancient societies and groups. One of the common threads through all of these examples is that there are similar conditions that are required for an initiation to be considered valid.

In his paper "The Meaning of Initiation," [1] Frank C. Higgins writes of various examples of how ancient candidates were prepared for initiation. He also provides us with insight into various initiatory practices. We often find three specific conditions that are common in what is considered valid initiation.

These three conditions are, a desire to initiate, a desire to be initiated, and the proper setting. If we look at a Masonic Lodge and examine how we initiate candidates we can find the same three conditions of initiation in practice in our Lodges.

When a candidate petitions to join Masonry, this is the desire to be initiated. He has taken an active step of his own free will. When a Lodge ballots on and accepts a petition, this is the desire to initiate. The proper setting of a Lodge is when an initiation takes place with the membership being respectful of the initiation and void of humor or distracting side discussions.

There is a thought that when one receives a proper initiation, a door is opened for them. But a door to what? The suggestion is that the door leads to another room ... a symbolic room of enlightenment, spiritual growth, and wisdom. But initiation itself does not give us these things, it only makes them available.

Rosicrucian philosophy speaks of one identified as the *Dweller on the Threshold.* This individual stands in an open doorway, but he does not enter the next room. He stands outside of the room filled with wonderful things. He does not take advantage of any of it by simply taking the next step of walking into the room.

Initiation is not the end goal for the true Seeker of Light. Initiation only opens the door for us. To receive any benefits from initiation, it is necessary for us to walk in and use the initiation as a means of advancing ourselves and gaining enlightenment. The responsibility of action is ours.

Wisdom through initiation was often a lifelong process for the initiates in many of the ancient enlightened cultures. A great center of wisdom was Alexandria, Egypt. Every imaginable area of enlightened study was available to students in Alexandria. Alexandria was located on the main trade routes and the area brought in many seeking greater knowledge of the Esoteric Arts. The hidden and reserved teachings from around the world were gathered together, studied, and preserved in Alexandria.

There was another important aspect of Alexandria. It was the large complex of libraries. The Libraries of Alexandria are the most famous in antiquity and most likely the largest ever assembled in ancient times. The libraries are said to have contained over a million documents containing the wisdom of the ancient worlds. When these libraries were destroyed, humanity was deprived of more knowledge than we can possibly ever realize. The destruction of these libraries also sealed off from us the source of the wisdom contained in these libraries. It is very possible that the source of the wisdom contained in these libraries were the libraries themselves. Enlightened initiates may have used these libraries not only as a source of knowledge, but as research centers where theories could be studied and developed.

But all that remains today are rumors, stories, and fables about the libraries and through them, with them, and because of them, the Ancient Mystery Schools.

In his paper, "The Egyptian Influence in our Masonic Ceremonial and Ritual"[2] Thomas Ross makes a very good point early in the paper. He notes that it was not until the early 1800s that any serious attempt at studying the Egyptian hieroglyphics was made. This presents us with the obvious question that if so little was known of Ancient Egyptian ritual at the foundation and early days of Speculative Freemasonry, then why does so much of our ritual so closely resemble Ancient Egyptian ritual? Where did the early Speculative Freemasons derive this knowledge? Suggestions that it could be coincidence borders on the irrational. Even the mention of the Ancient Mystery Schools in our Masonic teachings suggest some tie to the schools. And what is the tie? Initiation.

Given the vast amount of what we do not know of our early history, I do not feel that it is that great of a leap to suggest that ancient teachings, including those of initiation, traveled down through ancient times, through the Operative Masons and developed into what we know as Speculative Freemasonry.

The Ancient Mystery Schools can be looked at as a collection of formal, or informal, bodies of esoteric instruction. We can assume that in order to gain admission to one of these schools a candidate would need to pass through a rigorous screening and examination into their character. Following an examination into their worthiness they would take part in an initiation or some form of a Rite of Passage.

We can look at so many aspects of our Masonic initiation as well as our Masonic philosophy and teachings, and realize that so much of it is archaic. Our settings, furniture, symbols, words, and practices do seem to come from a different place and time. It is not difficult to see the similarities between our Hiramic legend and the legend of Osiris. It is not difficult to see many ancient teachings, traditions and symbols borrowed by Freemasonry from long-lost civilizations. But what were these civilizations?

Based on new discoveries and research our understanding of Ancient Egypt would seem to be in need of complete reexamination and rethought. Its level of scientific expertise and cultural development appear to be much greater than what is accepted by classical academia. Look at the massive and perplexing Sphinx. It was built during a time when there was not supposed to be any civilization in the area at all. What technology was there in place at the time of the building of the Sphinx? We have no idea. Look at what we know of very early Egyptian language, religion, and philosophy.

At what seems to be the beginning of the Old Kingdom and the first pharaohs we see there an intact hieroglyphic system, which was their complete writing system. We also see a complex science, religion and philosophy. Their whole system seems to have been there at the very beginning of the Old Kingdom. How is that possible? How is it possible to begin something as complex as the ancient Egyptian society with everything in place at the very beginning?

Rare and very early documents suggest much older advanced civilizations existing long prior to the time of the Old Kingdom. Maybe these older civilizations contributed to what would become their language and society. These very ancient and advanced civilizations may have been responsible for the building of many of the wonderful structures attributed to Dynastic Egypt. Clearly there is so very much that we simply do not know.

In his paper, "Rosicrucianism in Freemasonry,"[3] Harold Van Buren Voorhis tells us of the often misunderstood and equally mysterious Rosicrucians – the famous Brotherhood of the Rosy Cross. For the uninitiated, it is said that to try and understand the Rosicrucians is to try and grab handfuls of smoke. While it is sometimes difficult to sort the history from the lore, there are certain aspects of the Rosicrucians that we can look at and study … from a certain perspective.

Rosicrucianism has long been associated with both Freemasonry and the Ancient Mystery Schools. It has been suggested that the Rosicrucians and the Freemasons are something of first cousins. The fact is that trying to understand the early history of the Rosicrucians is as difficult as trying to understand the early history of Freemasonry. While the history of both Orders is obscured and difficult to impossible to completely understand, there is a thread that runs through the philosophy of both Orders that is kindred and somewhat traceable.

An old Rosicrucian thought is that either one has always been a Rosicrucian or they never will be one. While this statement makes no sense from an organizational standpoint, if we look at it from a philosophical view, then it takes on new meaning. The suggestion would seem to be that it is the Rosicrucian philosophy, not the organization, that is at the heart of being a Rosicrucian.

One is a Rosicrucian if they embrace its philosophy. Like Freemasonry, the Rosicrucian philosophy seems to have a life of its own separate and apart from the organization. Also like Freemasonry, the Rosicrucian Order has a distinct Egyptian flavor to it. Much of its philosophy, rituals, symbols, teachings, and even art are Egyptian in nature.

Again like Freemasonry, the Rosicrucian Order draws an association between itself and a particular medieval order, the Knights Templer. The Rose Croix, the Rosy Cross, the Order Rosae Crucis — all with the same theme, design, and suggestion — the Order of the Red Cross. But there is no clear answer as to why. Faint lines, rarely traceable do seem connect these secretive Orders, and for those capable of connecting obscured dots, trace what we have today, through esoteric philosophy, to the very early days of man. And what connects them all is initiation.

In very Ancient Egypt, the All-Seeing Eye was known as the Eye of Horus or the Eye of Ra. Through various myths this was a symbol of healing, protection, and wisdom. The left eye of Horus was said to be the moon and the right eye the sun. Some have suggested that the right and left "all-seeing eyes" reflect the two known decedents of the Ancient Mystery Schools: the Rosicrucians and the Freemasons.

If the suggestion is that the Ancient Mystery Schools, the great Temple at Karnack, transformed from a place of esoteric instruction into an active Order with the goal or preserving sacred wisdom and transmitting to it to future generations, then it is not difficult to see a very unscientific and unproven chain of transmission.

We can see early Jewish and Christian mystery traditions, including (but hardly limited to) the Nazarenes, the Essenes, the Jacobites, the Templars, the Operative Masons, the Rosicrucians, and Speculative Freemasonry — all passing on a secret tradition, a wisdom, a philosophy to future generations of initiates.

It would be naïve to suggest that we have many, if any, real answers. It would seem that we can be likened to a fully grown man with a rich, full history, but one with amnesia. All the details of his life would exist, but they would be unknown to him. But this is only when we examine Ancient Egyptian traditions. Ancient Eastern traditions also exist. The Hindus and Buddhists and many others also have rich esoteric traditions. In India, an ancient Sanskrit text informs us that the Hindu god Shiva has three eyes. One Rosicrucian writer suggests that this third all Seeing Eye reflects in Western esoteric tradition the triad of the Western Ancient Mystery Schools which include the Rosicrucians, the Freemasons, and ... the Roman Catholic Church. All three have ceremonies of initiation, teach through symbolic lessons, and preserve wisdom to pass on to future generations. Is any of this provable through scientific examination? Not at all. But prove that you love the Almighty. There are limits as to what can be proven through science, but no limits as to what is acceptable to a belief.

The poet Khalil Gibran once wrote, "Faith is a knowledge within the heart, beyond the reach of proof." We must have science to keep us grounded in reality, but if we are to have true balance than we must also have the creative imagination of a child and the courage to believe, even if what we believe cannot be proven through science.

If Freemasonry is only a club for the social enjoyment of our members, and if our ceremonies of initiation are only plays designed to entertain and mimic things that we don't understand, then nothing that we do is of any great importance. We might as well entertain ourselves in better ways. Certainly there are many more ways that we can entertain ourselves that are more satisfying than listening to minutes or arguing over the best ploy to attract new members.

But if Freemasonry is more than a club than maybe it is worth a closer look. I believe that we are much more than a club. I believe that initiation is that element within us that not only ties us to the Ancient Mystery Schools, but makes the past as relevant today as it was in ancient times. I believe that our Masonic initiation, when properly done, opens that mystic or spiritual door for us and gives us the opportunity to explore much deeper aspects of ourselves.

It's up to us if we want to walk through that door leading to deeper corners of ourselves, enlighten ourselves, explore ourselves, and grow to our limits. No one will force us. In fact, many times only few are aware of exactly what we have in our initiations. They are themselves as the Dweller on the Threshold – at best!

We must understand that there are times when our leaders and teachers are woefully ignorant of the treasure that is at our fingertips. It doesn't matter who is at fault for this situation. It simply exists.

There are a few things sadder than seeing the opportunity of initiation wasted because individuals, with no clue as to the true nature of Freemasonry, use our ceremonies as sources of entertainment. A side conversation about someone's cousin or brother who is down with the flu, or a traffic ticket they received that they believe was wholly unfair are nothing but violent weapons destroying the opportunity for a valid initiation.

The candidate may not be aware that anything has gone wrong, but he will also likely not be aware of that special something that many candidates feel when initiation is done properly. Placing blame and insulting either the unknowing or the knowing who allowed the levity or distractions is of little benefit. We must see Masonic initiation as a responsibility, an honor and a gift that we have to share.

Learning all the words of Masonic ritual will not guarantee a successful initiation. In fact, even if the Lodge does everything correctly a valid initiation may not take place if the candidate's mind is not prepared for the initiation. Making a good meal requires that all of the good ingredients be added in the right measure, cooked at the proper temperature, and for the proper length of time. But all of this will be a waste if the one eating the meal is ill and not capable of enjoying it.

What we have in Freemasonry is clearly very old. It has been clearly very important to many people for a very long time. This does not mean that we can prove an actual lineage to anything. If we believe the skeptics, there may be actually nothing of any value in an initiation – no matter if it is done properly or improperly.

On the other hand, maybe it is far more important, far older and far more significant than we have any idea. I for one believe that valid Masonic initiation is one of the keys to a rewarding life. In all aspects of the Lodge (as well as in all other Masonic bodies), we are to show respect, care and reverence.

I believe that we have either always been a Freemason, or that we never will be one.

Notes:

1. Higgins, Frank C. "The Meaning of Initiation." *Masonic Enlightenment: The Philosophy, History and Wisdom of Freemasonry.* Ed. Michael R. Poll. New Orleans, LA: Cornerstone Book Publishers, 2006. pp 18-21.

2. Ross, Thomas. "The Egyptian Influence in our Masonic Ceremonial and Ritual." *Masonic Enlightenment: The Philosophy, History and Wisdom of Freemasonry*. Ed. Michael R. Poll. New Orleans, LA: Cornerstone Book Publishers, 2006. pp 105-113.

3. Voorhis, Harold Van Buren. "Rosicrucianism in Freemasonry." *Masonic Enlightenment: The Philosophy, History and Wisdom of Freemasonry*. Ed. Michael R. Poll. New Orleans, LA: Cornerstone Book Publishers, 2006. pp 143-150.

More Masonic Books from Cornerstone

The Three Distinct Knocks
by Samuel Pritchard
6x9 Softcover 100 pages
ISBN 1613421826

Jachin and Boaz
by Samuel Pritchard
6x9 Softcover 92 pages
ISBN 1613421834

An Encyclopedia of Freemasonry
by Albert Mackey
Revised by William J. Hughan and Edward L. Hawkins
Foreword by Michael R. Poll
8.5 x 11, Softcover 2 Volumes 960 pages
ISBN 1613422520

Outline of the Rise and Progress of Freemasonry in Louisiana
by James B. Scot
Introduction by Alain Bernheim
Afterword by Michael R. Poll
8x10 Softcover 180 pages
ISBN 1-934935-31-X

In His Own (w)Rite
by Michael R. Poll
6×9 Softcover 176 pages
ISBN: 1613421575

Seeking Light
The Esoteric Heart of Freemasonry
by Michael R. Poll
6×9 Softcover 156 pages
ISBN: 1613422571

Cornerstone Book Publishers
www.cornerstonepublishers.com

More Masonic Books from Cornerstone

Masonic Enlightenment
The Philosophy, History and Wisdom of Freemasonry
Edited by Michael R. Poll
6 x 9 Softcover 180 pages
ISBN 1-887560-75-0

Morgan: The Scandal That Shook Freemasonry
by Stephen Dafoe
Foreword by Arturo de Hoyos
6x9 Softcover 484 pages
ISBN 1-934935-54-9

Masonic Questions and Answers
by Paul M. Bessel
6 x 9 Softcover 144 pages
ISBN 1-887560-59-9

Our Stations and Places - Masonic Officer's Handbook
by Henry G. Meacham
Revised by Michael R. Poll
6 x 9 Softcover 164 pages
ISBN: 1-887560-63-7

Knights & Freemasons: The Birth of Modern Freemasonry
By Albert Pike & Albert Mackey
Edited by Michael R. Poll
Foreword by S. Brent Morris
6 x 9 Softcover 178 pages
ISBN 1-887560-66-1

Robert's Rules of Order: Masonic Edition
Revised by Michael R. Poll
6 x 9 Softcover 212 pages
ISBN 1-887560-07-6

More Masonic Books from Cornerstone

The Freemasons Key
A Study of Masonic Symbolism
Edited by Michael R. Poll
6 x 9 Softcover 244 pages
ISBN: 1-887560-97-1

The Ancient and Accepted Scottish Rite in Thirty-Three Degrees
by Robert B. Folger
Introduction by Michael R. Poll
ISBN: 1-934935-88-3

The Bonseigneur Rituals
Edited by Gerry L. Prinsen
Foreword by Michael R. Poll
8x10 Softcover 2 volumes 574 pages
ISBN 1-934935-34-4

A.E. Waite: Words From a Masonic Mystic
Edited by Michael R. Poll
Foreword by Joseph Fort Newton
6 x 9 Softcover 168 pages
ISBN: 1-887560-73-4

Freemasons and Rosicrucians - the Enlightened
by Manly P. Hall
Edited by Michael R. Poll
6 x 9 Softcover 152 pages
ISBN: 1-887560-58-0

Masonic Words and Phrases
Edited by Michael R. Poll
6 x 9 Softcover 116 pages
ISBN: 1-887560-11-4

More Masonic Books from Cornerstone

Historical Inquiry into the Origins of the Ancient and Accepted Scottish Rite
by James Foulhouze
Foreword by Michael R. Poll
6x9 Softcover 216 pages
ISBN 1-613420-26-9

A General History of Freemasonry
by Emmanuel Rebold
Translated by J. Fletcher Brennan
Softcover 434 pages
ISBN 1-934935-81-6

Lectures of the Ancient and Primitive Rite of Freemasonry
by John Yarker
6x9 Softcover 218 pages
ISBN 1-934935-10-7

The Schism Between the Scotch & York Rites
by Charles Laffon de Ladébat
6x9 Softcover 66 pages
ISBN 1-934935-33-6

The Ceremony of Initiation
by W.L. Wilmshurst
6x9 Softcover 74 pages
ISBN 1-934935-02-6

The Master Workman or True Masonic Guide
by Henry C. Atwood
6x9 Softcover 396 pages
ISBN 1613420528

More Masonic Books from Cornerstone

A Concise History Of Freemasonry
by Robert Freke Gould
6×9, Softcover 468 pages
ISBN 1613422504

A Lexicon of Freemasonry
by Albert G. Mackey
6×9 Softcover 530 pages
ISBN 1613422202

Collected Essays
& Papers Relating to Freemasonry
by Robert Freke Gould
8.5×11 Softcover 340 pages
ISBN 1613422121

10,000 Famous Freemasons
by William Denslow
Foreword by Harry S. Truman
Cornerstone Foreword by Michael R. Poll
6×9, 4 Vol. Softcover 1,515 pages
ISBN 1-887560-31-9

The Ritual of the Operative Free Masons
by Thomas Carr
6×9 Softcover 66 pages
ISBN 1613421362

The Four Old Lodges
Founders of Modern Freemasonry and their Descendants
by Robert Freke Gould
8.5×11 Softcover 98 pages
ISBN 1613421001

Cornerstone Book Publishers
www.cornerstonepublishers.com

New Orleans Scottish Rite College

http://www.youtube.com/c/NewOrleansScottishRiteCollege

Clear, Easy to Watch
Scottish Rite and Craft Lodge
Video Education

Made in the USA
Middletown, DE
16 September 2017